D0942015

FAREWELL, PROMISED LAND

"Lake Moola" billboard, Valhalla trailer court, West Sacramento, 1993

FAREWELL, PROMISED LAND

Waking from the California Dream

ROBERT DAWSON AND GRAY BRECHIN

UNIVERSITY OF CALIFORNIA PRESS   BERKELEY   LOS ANGELES   LONDON

University of California Press

Berkeley and Los Angeles, California

University of California Press, Ltd.

London, England

© 1999 by

The Regents of the University of California

Library of Congress Cataloging-in-Publication Data

Dawson, Robert, 1950–

　　Farewell, promised land: waking from the California Dream /

　　Robert Dawson and Gray Brechin.

　　　　p.　cm.

　　Includes bibliographical references and index.

　　ISBN 0-520-21123-5 (cloth: alk. paper). — ISBN 0-520-21124-3

　　(pbk.: alk. paper)

　　　　1.　California—Environmental conditions.　　2.　California—

　　Environmental conditions—Pictorial works.　　3.　Environmental

　　management—California.　　I.　Brechin, Gray A.　　II.　Title.

　　GE155.C2D38　　1999

　　363.7′009794 — dc21　　　　　　　　　　　　　　98-24030

　　　　　　　　　　　　　　　　　　　　　　　　　　CIP

Printed in Italy

9　8　7　6　5　4　3　2　1

This book is printed on acid-free paper.

The publisher gratefully acknowledges the generous
contributions toward the publication of this book
provided by the following organizations and individuals:

The LEF Foundation
The Strong Foundation for Environmental Values
Richard M. Davis
Alice Q. Howard
Paul Sack

The publisher also gratefully acknowledges the
contribution provided by the General Endowment
Fund of the University of California Press.

For Walker Manchester Dawson and his generation.

— ROBERT DAWSON

To my brother Vern, who gave me the tools with which to write and teach.

— GRAY BRECHIN

CONTENTS

Raymond F. Dasmann

Farewell, Promised Land awakens far too many poignant memories of places we have lost. They have been taken away, one way or another—filled in, paved over, drained, torn down, burned out—inevitably crowded out. Too much has been removed from the wild—made tame or destroyed. I thought we had reached a low point thirty years ago when my book *The Destruction of California* was published. I actually hoped it would help to stop the downward trend. But nothing has halted the flood of people moving into California. Where one person stood thirty years ago there are now two. Where there was one when I was a child there are now twelve. They all take up space, demand housing, and need cars and highways, water development, sewage treatment, and so on—an interminable list of needs and wants. So the wild retreats vanish, often only in small increments, an easily ignored acre here and there, but collectively they add up to major losses.

Still, there is a California that is worth saving. Despite the losses, even more has been maintained. Battles have been lost, but the war can still be won. Those who are willing to work to preserve nature have more allies than ever before. I am optimistic enough to believe that *Farewell, Promised Land* can make a difference. It combines the visual impact of impressive photography with well-chosen words more successfully than any previous work.

Change is inevitable. Even the most carefully protected forest will not be quite the same tomorrow as it is today. But change can be positive, moving toward maintenance and restoration, and in that is our greatest hope. Cut-over forests need not remain as wasteland but can become forests once more. Overgrazed grasslands need not turn into desert but can regain their former luxuriance. It takes time and more patience than humans usually display, but recovery is always possible. If the seed stock has been maintained and soil kept in place, recovery can be relatively rapid. If much has been lost, it will take longer, but as long as biological diversity is maintained even barren lava beds can be green again.

The house that I lived in as a child in San Francisco was framed with old-growth Douglas fir. No doubt it was badly shaken in the 1906 earthquake, but it survived in good shape. The trees that produced its timbers, however, go much farther back; they were certainly growing when Cabrillo "discovered" California in 1542.

Nature has its own timetable, and people have trouble adjusting to it. I have yet to hear of a forest industry with the thousand-year cutting cycle needed to regrow the ancient redwoods that we so casually have removed from our forests.

Perhaps the change in our attitudes toward nature called for by *Farewell, Promised Land* is what is needed. I see it beginning to happen. One of my dreams has been to create a green ring of natural parks and reserves surrounding the urbanized areas of the San Francisco Bay region. When I look at a map I see that many of the reserves are already in place. They need only to be connected, as in the Golden Gate Biosphere Reserve, so that wildlife can move from one to another. The protection that already exists did not depend necessarily on the actions of Congress or the state legislature. Private individuals and organizations such as the Nature Conservancy, Trust for Public Land, Peninsula Open Space Trust, Sempervirens Fund, Save-the-Redwoods League, and many others have put up the money or brought pressure on the city and county governments to create parks and reserves.

The process of recovery and restoration goes on. Admittedly, the losses still tend to outweigh the gains. But I see hope in many things. Nature is reversing our past destruction of natural environments by reinvading lands now occupied by our cities. Each night in our backyard in Santa Cruz I see possums, skunks, gray foxes, and raccoons; once I even saw a bobcat. Deer feed on our front lawn. Not all of our neighbors are overjoyed to see these old residents returning. But attitudes are changing, and there is hope that Robert Dawson and Gray Brechin, with their sad farewell to California, will help bring a new dawn to this green and golden state.

Robert Dawson

Driving toward Stanford University, I listen to a new song by Bruce Springsteen about my childhood home in California's Central Valley. As I pass the Stanford Equestrian Center the ballad plays:

> Word was out some men in from Sinaloa were looking for hands
> Well deep in Fresno County there was a deserted chicken ranch
> There in a small tin shack on the edge of a ravine
> Miguel and Louis stood cooking methamphetamine

I think back three months, when Gray Brechin and I were working on this project in the San Joaquin Valley. We read in the local newspaper that the San Joaquin had become the meth capital of the country and about out-of-the-way farm shacks accidentally exploding during illegal drug production. We talked much about the desperation of the people caught up in this illicit drug world and the poverty that we saw every time we got off the freeways.

> It was early one winter evening as Miguel stood watch outside
> When the shack exploded lighting up the valley night
> Miguel carried Louis's body over his shoulder down a swale
> To the creekside and there in the tall grass Louis Rosales died[1]

Passing by the Stanford Golf Course, I weave through the slim joggers and determined mountain bikers who dominate the campus on this warm winter day. I think back to the California of my childhood and I am astonished at how dramatically this place has changed during my forty-five years in the Promised Land.

In 1991, Gray and I received the Dorothea Lange–Paul Taylor Prize from the Center for Documentary Studies at Duke University. We had talked about doing a book and exhibition on California's environment for years and were delighted that we had won the prize but horrified that now we would have to get to work.

Indirectly, we had been working on this project for a long time. Both of us were involved in the early effort to save eastern California's endangered Mono Lake, and had, in fact, met at a campground overlooking it. I went on to do a book with Gerald Haslam and Stephen Johnson on California's equally threatened agricultural heartland, the Great Central Valley. Later my wife, Ellen Manchester, and I cofounded a large collaborative photographic project called Water in the West that continues to look at water as a critical component of life throughout the arid West. Around 1989, Lonny

Shavelson and I photographed toxic waste sites throughout California. Gray was a cofounder of the Mono Lake Committee before moving to San Francisco to cover urban design and environmental issues for local magazines and television stations. In 1983 he helped to break the story of the poisoning of Kesterson National Wildlife Refuge.

Attending the University of California in the late 1960s and early 1970s, we were both shaped by the idealism of that time. *The Destruction of California* by Ray Dasmann (1965) helped both of us to understand the radical environmental transformation taking place around us. Dasmann's book was to California what Rachel Carson's *Silent Spring* (1962) was to the nation. It stuck with us both, becoming more relevant as the decades passed. We wanted to update it, but also to search the past for the explanations for California's continuing decline.

The way in which the United States came to occupy this land still affects the character of California society today. The California Gold Rush of 1849 was one of the largest mass migrations in human history and had enormous consequences for our environment and native life. Miner Thomas Swain wrote in 1851, "Large cities have sprung into existence almost in a day. . . . It has generally been the emigration of individuals, not of families. The people have been to each other strangers in a strange land. . . . Their hearts have been left at home. They have considered that as this is but a temporary stopping place for them, they have not been called upon to do anything for California but all for themselves." Another miner wrote, "Money is our only stimulus and getting of it our only pleasure," while Henry David Thoreau declared in 1862, "The rush to California . . . reflects the greatest disgrace on mankind. That many are ready to live by luck and so get the means of commanding the labor of others less lucky, without contributing any value to soci-ety—and that's called enterprise!" If only they could see us now.[2]

The visible changes in California's environment are there to see for all who can remember. The writer Joan Didion recalled growing up in Sacramento by noting: "All that is constant about the California of my childhood is the rate at which it disappears."[3] I, too, have spent a lifetime watching new homes spread over once-open land. Air quality has improved over parts of the state because of federal legislation in the 1970s, but the continued choking smog over southern California and parts of the Central Valley, the growing gridlocked traffic, and the fear that our state's population could double in twenty-five years fuels a persistent, underlying anxiety over California's future. The list of environmental disasters is long, and it is questionable whether our successes can be sustained over time as more people demand more of the land.

Our challenge was not only to depict the obvious crisis in our state but to remind people how we arrived here. What could we learn from our past to help us understand our present and redirect our future? Certain pivotal questions began to emerge.

Why has California allowed so much of its native plant and wildlife to be all but wiped out?

Can we really expect technology and chemically intensive agriculture to sustain us after we pave over the best of our farm land?

During the largely unknown nineteenth-century genocide of California's Indians, were we establishing an attitude of ownership, free of all constraints, which continues today on our land and among disenfranchised people?

Did James Marshall and the Gold Rush of 1849 lead to the cutting of the last old-growth forests and the death of our fisheries in the 1990s?

Has the California Dream of unlimited possibilities given us the propensity to build homes on flood plains, in fire zones, and over known earthquake faults?

To understand California's environmental crisis, it became imperative to understand what created the myth of California as America's Promised Land.

As a photographer, I was challenged by the task of making images of things that, in many cases, no longer exist. As we sought to understand the California Dream, I frequently encountered the question, how does one photograph history? Monuments, and the lack of them, gave us our cue. Early in the project we came upon a monument in the impoverished Sacramento / San Joaquin Delta town of Pittsburg. It depicted an old Italian fisherman gathering his nets and was dedicated to the last commercial fisherman in the Delta. On the coast, a hand-painted sign near Half Moon Bay perfectly conveyed the complex relationship between rapacious logging and California's all-but-extinct salmon runs. Near Los Angeles, we found a house-size section of the St. Francis Dam a mile downstream from its original site. The dam collapsed in 1928, taking hundreds of lives. No official monument exists marking this tragic event, yet this mass of concrete and rebar unofficially speaks volumes about what is often left out of history and why. Farther north, a private monument on a wind-swept, sun-baked plain in the Sacramento Valley spoke of how soldiers there controlled most of northern California's "militant" starving Indians in the 1850s. Never did we visit a more sorrowful place.

History began to emerge from plaques placed like epitaphs on our state's lonely monuments and memorials. Some bear official accounts erected by government or private groups. Some convey unofficial messages from concerned individuals. Other important sites, like the dam, have no monument at all. What has been commemorated and what has been left out prove to be revealing of our selective process of writing history. These plaques also provided me with the physical evidence I needed as a photographer. Gradually, the mist of California's myths began to clear as we stood in the place of so many tragic events. By bearing witness to this public history we sought to chronicle the origins of the Golden State's environmental decline. Recovering our dim memory of California's transformation became a central feature of our collaboration.

Gray and I worked well together, and the final project is greater than the sum of our individual efforts. As we shared our perspectives over meals, and while driving over long stretches of highway and back roads, we played off one another. Gray wrote to my photography and my photographs were informed by his thoughts. Traveling together through California's landscape, and visiting its archives, was a continual process of revelation, interpretation, and reexamination of a land in which we have spent our lives. Our project succeeded because we informed, motivated, and challenged each other in our effort to understand the familiar geography of our native state.

The book *California Historical Landmarks*, produced by the state's Office of Historic Preservation, provided invaluable assistance in helping us locate landscapes of historical environmental significance. The Federal Writers' Project's classic *WPA Guide to California* offered insight into the 1930s California landscape, and Stanford University Press's *Historic Spots in California* also gave us a map to follow history. The Nature Conservancy's *California Wild Lands* described and located the conservancy's remnant natural landscapes and gave us a glimpse of the remains of what once was California. DeLorme's road maps showed us the way.

It quickly became clear to us that depicting only devastation would invite cynicism and detachment. I felt it was essential to go beyond showing our failures by calling attention to individual and collective efforts to restore and sustain our home. People involved in preserving California are engaged in a struggle that agriculturist Wes Jackson once described as "becoming native" to a place. Jackson argues that our culture has settled on the American landscape but that we have yet to become native to that place we call home. That process of becoming native motivates many of the people and organizations in our book. In undertaking this project, we too were searching for a way to come home.

We spent most of 1995 traveling to every region of the state. During that time it occurred to us to include a chapter depicting "alternative courses," as we discovered a rich history of Californians trying to create communities outside the mainstream. Utopian communities such as socialist Llano del Rio and Kaweah tried and ultimately failed to redefine our basic economic system. A nineteenth-century community of former slaves in Tulare County, now identified as Colonel Allensworth State Historic Park, attempted to provide a place for disenfranchised blacks to join the Central Valley's farm economy. The early twentieth-century town of Runnymede (now East Palo Alto) bore the motto "One Acre and Independence." A few years ago it became the "murder capital of the country." Yet Trevor Burrowes worked with residents there to grow commercially valuable organic vegetables on the original one-acre lots to break the cycle of poverty. Contemporary alternative communities continue to seek paths away from our apparent environmental suicide.

Amid all the bad news we found signs of hope in individuals and organizations actively engaged in the task of restoring where they live. From river restoration in Los Angeles to community restoration in San Francisco, we discovered Californians who have dedicated their lives to rehabilitating their communities and preserving a sense of unique place against the onslaught of development. As wealth becomes increasingly concentrated, many people feel increasingly insignificant and powerless, but those we interviewed proved that individual efforts can still make a difference.

I also photographed remnant natural landscapes to remind us of what we have lost. Several of these sites were lands purchased by the Nature Conservancy, including remnants of the Central Valley natural landscape such as the Vina Plains Preserve, the Kaweah Oaks Preserve, the Pixley Vernal Pools Preserve, and the Jepson Prairie Preserve. The Carrizo Plain, just west of the San Joaquin Valley, has been called "California's Serengeti" because of its remaining prairie and wildlife. The Tule Elk State Reserve, west of Bakersfield, is attempting to bring back the once-abundant tule elk to its native home. The San Francisco Bay National Wildlife Refuge is the largest urban wildlife refuge in the country. Meanwhile, the Eastern Mojave continues to be a battleground over public versus private ownership of California's desert. The California State University system and the University of California are trying to retain a semblance of the original desert through their desert research stations in the Eastern Mojave.

None of these preserves would exist without the work of people who loved a particular place, or who had a larger vision of what California and its cities might become if nurtured with human wisdom. People continue to make a difference in their efforts to become native to California. We who have had the privilege to see the state whole hope that this book may serve as a window for other Californians, that they may be inspired to strive to turn the land we inhabit into home.

We are very grateful to the following people and organizations for helping us with this project.

The Center for Documentary Studies at Duke University awarded us the Dorothea Lange–Paul Taylor Prize to begin the project. Alex Harris and Iris Tilman Hill from the Center were early and enthusiastic supporters.

For their contributions to support the production of this volume, we thank the previously named donors, as well as Carolyn Abst, Nancy L. Blair, Robert A. Chlebowski, William T. Davoren, Jim and Louise Frankel, Robert C. Friese, Noel and Sandra Kirshenbaum, Ira Kurlander and Jim Mays, Martin and Joan Rosen, and Tova Wiley. We are also grateful to Grace and Ric de Laet, Elizabeth Marshall, and Jim Sotiros for making these contributions possible.

Professional Color Lab in San Francisco provided continued support. We received valuable assistance from Lighthawk and its pilots; Phil Mumma and the Oakland Museum; the Museum of Vertebrate Zoology at the University of California, Berkeley; the Foundation for Deep Ecology; the Institute for Historical Study; and the staffs of the Bancroft Library, Stanford Special Collections, California Historical Society, Library of Congress, National Maritime Museum, and California State Library. Special appreciation to Jennifer Watts of the Huntington Library for making our work so much easier.

The following individuals generously gave us their invaluable assistance: Ray Dasmann, Harold Gilliam, Michael Black, Rebecca Solnit, Judy Irving, Josh and Laurel Collins, Judith Marvin; our editors at the University of California Press, Sheila Levine, Valeurie Friedman, Rose Vekony, and Monica McCormick; Lee Swent, Sandra Phillips, Malcolm Margolin, Peter Palmquist, Tim Drescher, Topher Delaney, Richard Walker, Jim Parsons, Therese Heyman, Greg Garr, Larry Landis, Bryan Turner, Lloyd Carter; and Sid, Dyvonne, and Gwen Brechin. Special thanks to Bob Chlebowski for his unfailing patience, Ellen Manchester for her inspiration, and Martha and Bros. coffee for the fuel to get it all done.

Finally, we would like to acknowledge some of the often unsung people and groups working to save California's environment: Michael Abelman, the American Farmland Trust, Ruth Brinker, Trevor Burrowes, the late Aurora Castillo, Pratap Chatterjee, Henry Clark and the West County Toxics Coalition, Bill Davoren, Steve and Gloria Decater, the Friends of the Urban Forest, the Greenbelt Alliance, Luna Leopold, Lewis MacAdams, Sylvia McLaughlin, the Mono Lake Committee, the Nature Conservancy, Ann Riley, San Francisco Estuary Institute, the San Francisco League of Urban Gardeners (SLUG), Dave Simpson, Ted Smith, Cathrine Sneed, and Seth Zuckerman. You are an inspiration to us all.

Tolowot/
Indian
Island

COAST RANGE

Nomi
Lackee

Sacramento R.

SIERRA

Ukiah •
□ Bloody Island

Sacramento •
□ Jepson Prairie
• Delta

San
Francisco •
• Pittsburg

San Joaquin R.

NEVADA

Friant
Dam

COAST RANGE

PACIFIC OCEAN

• Hanford

Tulare Lake
• Pixley

Kern R.

Bakersfield •

Buena Vista Lake
Kern Lake

Tehachapi Mts.

□ Fort Tejon

MOJAVE DESERT

• Los Angeles
□ Saahatpa

□ Monument

0   50   100   150 miles

San Diego •

N

An Altered Land

Monarch, California's last wild grizzly and symbol for state flag,
California Academy of Sciences, San Francisco, 1996

ONE: THE ABSENCE OF THINGS

I noticed the emptiness of the sky long before I saw it on the land. Approaching Sacramento on the Yolo Causeway, I saw a sky free of motion. Where historic accounts spoke of torrents of birds so dense that they cast a shadow upon the ground, of thunderous rivers of geese, ducks, and swans moving down the state to the lagoons of Mexico and beyond, now there was nothing. Like most Californians, I'd come to take the emptiness for granted.

As a historian, I now see it everywhere—a growing and unseen poverty in the well-advertised land of plenty—and I know that we did it to ourselves. A 1901 photograph courtesy of the Southern Pacific promotional department showed men standing next to a trophy sea bass taller than themselves. The railroad hoped, through such publicity, to lure more settlers to the vast tracts of real estate that it claimed throughout the West. Because it worked so well, we will never see such fish again, or the state the *Chronicle* advertised in 1906 as "The Nation's Noah's Ark," telling sportsmen where they could bag the last of the big ones. Two years later, the same paper called the Colorado River delta the "best hunting and fishing in America," even as the diversions began that now exhaust the river long before it reaches the sea. The jungles and lagoons at its mouth on the Gulf of California have vanished. Hunters will never again pose for *Sunset* on a feathered mound of Canada geese brought down from the California skies. Little moves up there these days but the contrails of flying machines.

Humans are such an adaptable species that few are aware of the absence of animals with which they once shared the place. But far more than wildlife is missing from California today.

I was standing in the Jepson Prairie while Bob attempted to photograph its meagerness. The Nature Conservancy protects the 1,600 acres as the last and largest stand of native grasses left in the 15 million-acre Central Valley. Things have changed since John Muir described the valley's "bee pastures," where every footstep crushed a hundred flowers, "one sheet of purple and gold" sweeping from the Coast Range to the Sierra foothills "with the bright Sacramento pouring through the midst of it." Within decades of that first view, Muir wrote, the flowery pastures had vanished as if burned, retreating to "rocky cliffs and fencecorners." They were replaced by a sea of wheat and by rocky stubble where livestock grazed "like hoofed locusts."[1]

Yet as late as 1915, the San Francisco world's fair was tinted to resemble the spring wildflowers for which the state was still famous. Once again, the *Chronicle* featured an article on the wild "gardens" that grew on the dunes within the city limits, including the usual picture of a woman gathering armfuls of lupine for short-lived bouquets. The fair was, of course, designed to attract people to California to populate those fields, as was the article, since the newspaper's proprietor also owned blocks of those sand dunes. Both were successful, for a sea of houses and streets now covers every trace of what the *Chronicle* called "the most gorgeous expanse of natural bloom in California."

It takes a stretch of the imagination that I cannot muster to see the tiny relic of the Jepson preserve, with its hummocks, bunch grasses, and flower-edged ponds, extending from Shasta to the Tehachapis and hosting herds of antelope and elk. One is everywhere reminded of the meagerness of what once was, for Jepson is a prairie at tight bay. Closely bounded by a county road on one side and a railroad bed on the other, it is quartered by power pylons that stride across the landscape, carrying juice to the bay cities and the nearby Solano suburbs that threaten soon to engulf it. The pervasive crackling of overhead high voltage is itself drowned out, every few minutes, by the roar of huge transports cruising into Travis Air Force Base. Jepson is another one of those fence corners preserved in a landscape of utility because it is of little use for anything else. It speaks eloquently of a poverty of intention.

Arriving in California eighteen years before Muir, Thomas Jefferson Mayfield confirmed what the Scots naturalist reported. Mayfield never forgot his first view of the San Joaquin Valley when,

as a young boy, he hastened with his family to the gold fields of the Sierra. Standing on the Coast Range, he saw fields of living gold, and much more. His mother described it as "a crazy quilt of color," and his father, though well traveled, said he would not have believed that such a place existed had he not seen it himself. Descending to the plain, the Mayfields decked their horses with flowers. Many were unknown to them, since plants had evolved uniquely in the isolation of California as on an island, each attuned to local environmental nuances. Thomas recalled that "the whole plain was covered with great patches of rose, yellow, scarlet, orange and blue. The colors did not seem to mix to any great extent. Each kind of flower liked a certain kind of soil best and some of the patches of one color were a mile or more across." The memory never faded, for more than sixty years later, Mayfield recalled that "the two most

Opposite: *Ishi's urn, Colma, 1996*

Olcott Pool, Jepson Prairie, 1995

beautiful remembrances I have are the virgin San Joaquin and my mother." [2]

Contributing greatly to the beauty of the valley was the unbroken range of the Sierra Nevada, which walls it to the east and which the Mayfields at first mistook for a long bank of clouds. That view, too, is gone. "No quality of the air of California," wrote a correspondent for a mining magazine of 1883, "is more marked than its transparent clearness, especially during the greater part of winter and spring. In this regard, our Pacific atmosphere quite equals the noted Italian skies." [3]

Nineteenth-century travelers commonly likened the air, light, and landscape of California to that of the Mediterranean. Once, in Venice, I recalled their descriptions after a violent storm briefly ripped away the curtain of dirt that usually hides the mountains just to the north. Before that storm, I'd thought the Alps too far to be seen from the city, though maps showed their summits only sixty miles away—far closer than the Sierra peaks seen from the Coast Range. The Italian Renaissance artists who painted the Alps as a jagged blue backdrop to Venice must have used poetic license, I had thought, just as Muir must have exaggerated when he described the

"Farm Water 'Works'!" sign on dry Tulare lake bed, San Joaquin Valley (diptych), 1996

Sierra Nevada appearing, from the Coast Range, "not clothed with light, but wholly composed of it, like the wall of some celestial city."[4]

That storm in Venice revealed, once again, what has so gradually been lost everywhere. The correspondent of 1882 went on to praise the exceptionally fine view of the Sierra from the San Joaquin Valley. A woodcut illustration of 120 miles of mountains seen from the town of Hanford accompanied the description of what, today, is almost perpetually hidden by a dingy broth of smoke, exhaust, and dust that fills the basin of the San Joaquin.

Much of that dust comes from the bed of what was once the largest freshwater body west of the Great Lakes. It was formed by a broad alluvial fan near Hanford, which blocked the runoff of the Sierra Nevada from joining the San Joaquin River in its northward course to San Francisco Bay. The fan turned the Sierra's southernmost rivers to pond in an enclosed basin. Reed-rimmed Tulare Lake was the biggest of the terminal lakes, covering nearly 760 square miles in wet years; but farther to the south, beneath the granite peaks of the Tehachapis, lay the Kern and Buena Vista Lakes.

Today, the beds of those lakes are platted with a grid of fields and briny evaporation ponds filled with agricultural waste. Like the Colorado, the rivers are diverted in all but the wettest years to grow both cotton and cities. Drivers speeding between Los Angeles and the Bay Area on Interstate 5 are unaware that the featureless plain through which they move with such haste and boredom was once a vortex of life, a critical stop on the Pacific Flyway and, least of all, that in spring it could elicit cries of joy from those who first saw it. Few know that they are crossing a desert made by man, or that the dust in the air was largely caused by a water table now so depleted that the roots of plants can no longer reach it. Somewhere out there, a nineteenth-century artist drew an island covered with white pelicans.

The replacement of nature's diversity with the uniformity of the marketplace, or of the emptiness of the skies, is generally so gradual that few notice the change. In the case of the San Joaquin lakes, however, someone watched it happen. Bill Barnes was ninety in 1954, but his memory was still as sharp as Thomas Mayfield's when that local historian interviewed him.[5] Barnes remembered when two thousand antelopes came to drink at a water hole, and millions of birds congregated on Pelican Island to raise their young. Inland otters were plentiful then; Barnes hunted the tules and got three dollars for their skins.

While Barnes was trapping in the lakes, farmers were busy tapping the groundwater east of them. The San Francisco firm of Haggin & Tevis was taking the rivers to irrigate a half-million-acre barony it would later incorporate as the Kern County Land Company. The valley lakes were in the way, and around 1880 someone set fire to the tules around Tulare Lake, burning the organically rich soil down five or six feet. Starved of inflow, the lakes shrank. Millions of fish died on the mud, making a terrible stench, Barnes recalled, but the otters feasted for weeks. Then they too starved, and never returned. Raccoons moved in for their turn on the carcasses of the dead otters until nothing was left, and Barnes later watched thousands of them stagger about, emaciated, on the dry lake bed. The birds went elsewhere to starve. Then, there was silence. "The country was never the same afterward," he observed laconically.

Admittedly, along with the lakes went their mosquitoes, and with them the malaria introduced into California around 1830. Mayfield and Muir were fortunate enough to see the valley in the spring before the summer heat scorched its grasses. But embedded within

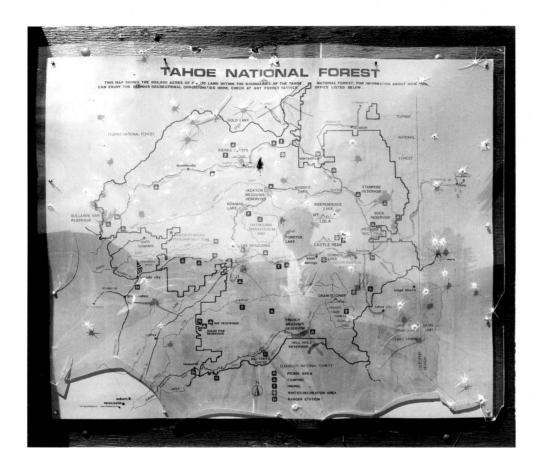

Bullet-riddled sign, Tahoe National Forest, 1988

Bill Barnes's description is a violence so commonplace that it is not recognized as such by those who wreak it. They once called it "improvement," but today we call it development.

The same soon happened to other critical habitats billed by the San Francisco press as paradises for sportsmen—the Colorado Delta on the Mexican border and Tule Lake next to Oregon, for example. Barnes, in the middle, witnessed the sudden collapse of one of the West's most productive ecosystems. Surveyors moved quickly onto the cracked mud bottoms of the lake, laying upon them the gridded landscape of real estate.[6] The destruction of Tulare Lake,

however, took more than pelicans, otters, elks, swans, herons, bears, eagles, clams, antelopes, and ducks with it. People went too, as little noticed as the animals on which they depended, the unwitting and unmourned victims of market forces in distant cities, and of the consoling ideology that might makes right.

Somewhere near Hanford, the Mayfield family established a homestead in the broad valley that Thomas's mother loved, and there she died. Unable or unwilling to care for his son, Thomas's father allowed nearby Indians to raise the boy as one of their own. For ten years, Thomas Jefferson Mayfield lived and played with the

Above: *Former Indian village site, Tunitas Creek, 1995*

Above right: *Abandoned Indian school, Fort Bidwell, 1995*

Captain Jack's Stronghold, Lava Beds National Monument, 1995

Choinumne, a subset of the Yokut people. He spoke their language and descended the Kings River with them in tule boats to hunt and fish in the Tulare Lake marshes. They made their last trip, he reckoned, in 1855. After that, settlers and soldiers crowded them into ever-dwindling and more barren reservations, together with their enemies and whiskey. The culture of the Choinumne, as closely attuned to the nuances of the valley as the wildflowers Mayfield observed, disintegrated long before the lake turned to dust and cotton. They died unseen, like the birds with whom they lived.

We found the same story repeated everywhere in California. At a rest stop provided by Caltrans to break the monotony of Highway 10 in Riverside County, few travelers read a monument commemorating the site of Saahatpa, a village of Indians who helped early settlers. There, says the plaque with unusual candor, "Cahuilla tradition asserts that the U.S. Government sent Army blankets that were contaminated with smallpox. After this disaster, Saahatpa was abandoned."

Such bacteriological warfare was not uncommon in a nation attempting to free the land of all impediments to material success. To the early settlers, the Indians were scarcely human, but more akin to beasts of no value, and as such, fit for sport and massacre. Few understood that the degraded condition of "the Diggers" was the result of poverty forcibly imposed. They became, in the most literal sense, fair game.

Thomas Jefferson Mayfield might have dissented, but he quickly learned to shut up. "I knew the Indians in their natural state and I know that they were the finest people that I have ever met," he said after spending more than sixty years back with his own kind. He found that those whites to whom he returned in 1862 were so ignorant that it was useless to challenge their certainty of their own superiority. Mayfield never mentioned his remarkable childhood experience until he found a sympathetic ear just before his death in 1928.

California's native people relied for their sustenance upon the bounty of a state whose rivers ran clear and unobstructed. That changed abruptly with the Gold Rush of which the Mayfield family was a part. A U.S. surveyor observed, "Never before in history has a people been swept away with such terrible swiftness, or appalled into utter and unwhispering silence forever, as were the California Indians . . . . Let a tribe complain that the miners muddied their salmon runs, or steal a few packmules, and in twenty days there might not be a soul of them living."[7]

The faces of those people stare out of old photographs as if from prison mug shots, weary, guarded, and infinitely sad for what they witnessed and endured. California was admitted to the Union in 1850 as a free state, with the exception of its native inhabitants whom the Constitution allowed whites to "indenture" under broadly drafted vagrancy laws. Only the ratification of the Fourteenth Amendment in 1868 curtailed what amounted to a legal slave trade in the Golden State.

A woman named Helen Carpenter recalled, in 1893, how hunters once combed the hills around Ukiah looking for special game. They sought children, whom they orphaned and brought to town to sell as houseworkers and field hands. The business was agreeably brisk, for the children did not live long in captivity, and more were always needed. Young girls made lucrative prostitutes.[8]

The state offered bounties for the scalps of Indians; those of women were worth less than men's, and those of children least of all. Shoved like the prairies into fence corners good for nothing else, survivors died where few would notice. One southern California

Above: *Site of Evans and Bailey fight in 1861, near Canby, 1995*

Above right: *Bloody Point, near Tule Lake, 1995*

Infernal Caverns Battleground grave markers, near Likely, 1995

Pioneer Monument, San Francisco, 1996

Fort Tejon, 1995

tribe had no choice but to sink a well through its ancestral burial mound. Another, noted a small *Chronicle* article of 1904, fought vultures for rotten food while waiting for government aid that did not come. Pomos in Lake County were given an abandoned mercury dump as a reservation.

Few places in California are as broodingly empty as Nomi Lackee. More than a hundred and forty years after the government designated it a camp for native people who were concentrated there from the Sacramento Valley, it is still far from anywhere. We found it in Tehama County on a fine spring morning after crossing the Coast Range. A farmer, seeing our confusion on a country road, took us there and left us in the silence.

The Indians driven to Nomi Lackee were allowed to live on the rolling grassland until it was taken by others with needs deemed more valid than theirs. The reservation was the northern counterpart of another, which Indian Superintendent Edward F. Beale sited at Tejon Pass in the Tehachapis for its inadequacy to support human life.[9] Indians starved in the north as they did at Fort Tejon, but at Nomi Lackee, subagent V. E. Geiger put them to use planting wheat on acreage that he then claimed as his own. Geiger indentured his wards to raise his crops and to care for the cattle he ran on their reservation. Beale, in the south, turned Fort Tejon and much more into a dynastic fiefdom called the Tejon Ranch with what one admiring visitor called its own peasantry of Indians. Both federal agents, in effect, converted their reservations into southern plantations.

By 1866, twelve years after its establishment, Nomi Lackee was officially privatized; soldiers drove those who survived across the

Former Indian reservation, Nomi Lackee (triptych), 1995

mountains in a nightmarish "trail of tears" to an even more remote outpost in Round Valley, where they have lived on uneasy terms with white settlers ever since.

Some places have drunk so much pain that they never give it up. We call them haunted. Nomi Lackee is one such place. A stillness hangs over the valley beyond the mere absence of animals once there. Even in the brightness of noon, an unseen cloud hangs over the land and strikes a chill in those who take the trouble to search it out. I felt that cold once before. It was outside the village of Dachau, in Germany.

How does one photograph an ecosystem that was suddenly ripped apart, and with it a people and their culture? The site of

Nomi Lackee is commemorated by a private monument, rising from a hillock in a field and surrounded by a railing of galvanized pipes. You could easily mistake the lone marker from a distance for a tombstone. Its inscription reads only: "Indian military post, 1854 – 1866. Nomi Lackee Indian Reservation controlled over 300 to 2,500 militant Indians. U.S. Survey of 1858 showed 25,139.71 acres in the reservation. Indians moved to Round Valley in 1866."

Above the inscription, a Conestoga wagon moves west in bas-relief. It was the Indians' misfortune to play the Canaanites in this Promised Land. The plaque was set there in 1938 by the Native Daughters of the Golden West to commemorate the state's romantic heritage.

Monument to site of first adobe home, Lake County, 1995

It is, of course, the victors' prerogative to rewrite history, and thus to delete what they do not wish themselves or their children to remember. California is rich in monuments that tell the story of those who won its land. But sometimes, they suggest the losers' side of the tale. Another plaque commemorates a slaughter that gave Bloody Island in Lake County its name. When Indians, in 1849, killed two white men who had brutally enslaved and tortured them, U.S. soldiers sought a vengeance as unfocused as it was enthusiastic. Under Infantry Captain N. Lyon, they cornered men, women, and children on an island at the north end of Clear Lake and systematically shot, stabbed, and clubbed an estimated hundred or more. To make sure they had punished the real perpetrators of the

View from Bloody Island, Lake County, 1995

Blood Scattered Like Water

From *Native American Testimony*, ed. Peter Nabokov, pp. 101–6 [10]

The Bloody Island Massacre of 1850 took place during the darkest period of California Indian history. Anti-Indian sentiment was at a fever pitch. Over the next two decades thousands of Native Americans— contemptuously termed Diggers—were killed by the military, by citizen-organized "Indian hunts," and by disease. Between 1850 and 1863 an estimated ten thousand California Indians—children preferred—were sold or indentured for cheap labor in the United States and Mexico.

Among such outrages was the murder of more than a hundred Pomo Indian men, women, and children on an island in Lake County's Clear Lake— "a perfect slaughter pen" in the words of the United States army officer whose troops did the deed.

Here Chief William Benson, born twelve years after the event, gives his people's version of what happened. It opens with the murder of Stone and Kelsey, two former trappers who had abused a band of starving, semi-enslaved Pomos. Attempting to rustle cattle to stay alive, the Indians accidentally lose their overseer's horse. Realizing they will be punished, they decide to kill Stone and Kelsey, their bosses. Although they flee, it is with a foreboding sense of the terrible retaliation that awaits them.

. . . "The next morning the white warriors came across in their long dugouts. The Indians said they would meet them in peace. So when the whites landed, the Indians went to welcome them but the white man was determined to kill them.

"Ge-Wi-Lih said he threw up his hands and said, 'No harm, me good man.' But the white man fired and shot him in the arm, and another shot came and hit a man standing along side of him and was killed. So they had to run and fight back; as they ran back in the tuleys [bulrushes] and hid under the water; four or five of them gave a little battle and another man was shot in the shoulder. Some of them jumped in the water and hid in the tuleys. Many woman and children were killed on [or] around this island.

"One old lady, a Indian told about what she saw while hiding under a bank under a cover of hanging tuleys. She said she saw two white men coming with their guns up in the air and on their guns hung a little girl. They brought it to the creek and threw it in the water. And a little later two more men came in the same manner. This time they had a little boy on the end of their guns and also threw it in the water. A little ways from her she said lay a woman shot through the shoulder. She held her little baby

in her arms. Two white men came running torge [toward] the woman and baby. They stabbed the woman and the baby and threw both of them over the bank in to the water. She said she heard the woman say, 'O my baby'; she said when they gathered the dead, they found all the little ones were killed by being stabbed, and many of the women were also killed [by] stabbing. She said it took them four or five days to gather up the dead: And the dead were all burnt on the side of the creek. . . .

"The next morning the soldiers started for Mendocino County. And there killed many Indians. The camp was on the ranch now known as Ed Howell ranch. The soldiers made camp a little ways below about one half mile from the Indian camp. The Indians wanted to surrender. But the soldiers did not give them time. The soldiers went in the camp and shot them down as if they were dogs. Some of them escaped by going down a little creek leading to the river. And some of them hid in the brush. And those who hid in the brush most of them were killed. And those who hid in the water was overlooked. They killed mostly women and children. . . ."

William Benson, Pomo

Indian / Gunther Island, National Historic Landmark, Eureka, 1995

crime, they proceeded down the Russian River to ambush and kill an additional 150 or so. After listing the bare facts of the Bloody Island massacre, the plaque adds that "doubt exists of these Indians' guilt."

Some memorials say nothing at all. At a marina on an island off the Eureka waterfront, an immense bronze statue of a man in a mackintosh honors local fishermen lost at sea. Nearby, yet another plaque commemorates something that existed or happened on an adjacent island in Humboldt Bay. Just what the viewer is asked to remember, however, is unclear, for the monument says only:

Indian/Gunther Island
Site 67 (Tolowot)
Has been designated a National Historic Landmark
This site possesses national significance in commemorating
the history of the United States of America.

On the night of February 25, 1860, while the men of Tolowot were away, the men of Eureka took the opportunity to burn the village and ax to death women, children, the old, and the infirm. The event was so shameful, so sadistic in its ferocity, that editor Bret Harte denounced it in his newspaper and was forced by the death threats that followed to hastily leave town. Lest anyone ask, the island took a new name from the man who subsequently claimed and sold it. That, we figured, is the event that the monument forgot to commemorate.

You have to crack eggs to make an omelet, or to make real estate, and as one of the world's most golden omelets, California is littered with the eggshells of massacres, lynchings, forced marches, and exterminations necessary to grid and market its land. So is the state rich in monuments whose silences tell far more about those who placed them than about the events that they do or do not choose to remember. As with the otters of Tulare Lake, no monuments commemorate the more common deaths by disease and starvation, or by despair. Mythologies, after all, are compounded as much by omission as by commission.

I mentioned Dachau. For those unfamiliar with the untold history of California, the analogy will, of course, seem extreme. U.S. policy toward the natives was contradictory and, occasionally, well intentioned. Yet incidents alone did not bring to mind that other "reservation" in Bavaria. Such sentiments as the following were not uncommon in the California press: "There is, perhaps, no doubt that the aboriginal race must disappear. . . . But it is our duty as a conquering, overpowering race to treat them gently—though it is now late to begin—and let them pass quietly away as Nature has ordained."[11]

Nature increasingly took the rap for what men had done, thus salving the conscience of those made queasy by the messy details of extermination and transformation. By 1890 the native population of California had dropped to 5 percent of what it had been a century earlier at the dawn of contact. The same 1915 world's fair whose brightly colored architecture recalled the vanishing flowers of California celebrated, too, the "tragedy of a dying race" with a statue that became an enduring national icon. James Earle Fraser's "The End of the Trail" was once paired with another statue that symbolized the triumph of the master race.

In the peaceful walled garden of Mission Dolores stand the individual tombstones of those settlers who left their names on San Francisco's streets, hills, and districts. Among them, a simple granite pedestal reads, "In Prayerful Memory of Our Faithful Indians"; it supports a statue of Tekakwitha, "The Lily of the Mohawks,"

"End of the Trail" statue with the man who posed for it, Panama-Pacific International Exposition, 1915 (courtesy California History Room, California State Library, Sacramento)

looking to her salvation in heaven. The shaft marks the grave of an estimated six thousand Californians whose identity, as at all other missions they once built, has been lost in such mass burials. Far more impressive than those anonymous lots is the recumbent statue of Father Junipero Serra at the Carmel Mission, his feet resting on a grizzly cub. Serra led the advance into California, and today advances toward sainthood for doing so.

Who really won, I wonder, in the violence that attended this triumphal march? A statue at the end of the main street of Pittsburg, at the point where the San Joaquin River once joined the Sacramento to flush the San Francisco Bay, tells more. There, an old but powerful Sicilian strains to pull in his net. A plaque says that it was placed there "In memory of the deltawaters pioneer fishermen" and sculpted by Frank J. Vitalie, the son of the man portrayed. It is subtitled "The Day the River Closed" and represents the weariness, resentment, and uncertainty felt by fishermen on that day in 1957 when the state outlawed commercial fishing on the delta to save what remained.

There is not room enough on the plaque to blame the Friant Dam that blocks the San Joaquin River, or a pumping plant upriver that drives the Sacramento River's fresh water south to the fields of the San Joaquin Valley. Nor is there room to mention the rain of chemicals necessary to create and sustain the Central Valley's monocultures, or the industrial and urban wastes fish must navigate as they enter the delta, or the shadeless channels, the weirs and walls of concrete they encounter before reaching their ancestral spawning grounds, usually now buried beneath deep draw-down reservoirs. There is no space for the piecemeal and radical rearrangement of California's hydrology, which contributed to the tragedy of an Italian-American family and all the others who once depended on fish for their livelihood. The once-mighty migrations of salmon have

Model of Old Mission Dolores, San Francisco, 1995

Father Serra's cenotaph with grizzly cub at Serra's feet, Carmel Mission, Carmel, 1995

Monument to the last commercial fisherman in the delta by Frank J. Vitalie, Pittsburg, 1992

withered as radically as the bird populations overhead, and twenty-foot-long sturgeon belong to the past; their departure has left human poverty for the "victors" as it once did for the vanquished.

The bitterness suggested in the statue's inscription is reflected in the closed storefronts of Pittsburg, which, like so many California towns, has the look of a place forgotten except by those who can-not escape it. Another such town is Pixley, two hundred miles south of the delta and just east of the bed of Tulare Lake. It's a tired place off the main highway, like scores of others, consisting of one main street with a Mexican restaurant, a bar, and a row of boarded-up stores. It, too, has a monument commemorating something no longer there.

Plaque explaining history of dry artesian wells, Pixley, 1992

Farm abandoned by falling water table, 1939 (courtesy Library of Congress)

A gray granite slab stands at the center of town with the head-line "Artesian Wells." It recalls the settlers who discovered an un-derground reservoir buried under such pressure that water gushed to the surface without pumping. Such wells were once common in California. By 1885, it says, farmers had drilled more than 250 wells. Drawing upon the accumulated capital of geologic ages, towns flourished for a few decades along the artesian belt from Han-ford to Earlimart. While the lake to the west dried up, farmers broke the sod and cut and burned the oak trees that had fed the Yokuts. The Southern Pacific Railroad took cash crops to the city.

And then, the text concludes abruptly, something went wrong: "By the first decade of the twentieth century most artesian water stopped flowing. Several explanations for this have been explored over the years."

The Tulare County Historical Society and the Pixley Women's Club dedicated the slab in 1989. It stands in a dry and cracked con-crete basin that was once the town's watering trough. The valley around Pixley has dropped about twenty feet since pumping began,

Clearcut of Spooner Summit, 1876 (photo by Carleton Watkins, collection of Peter Goin and William Bliss)

World's fair Big Tree. This is the largest piece of timber ever taken from California (courtesy Oakland Museum of California)

irreversibly compacting the aquifer that gave birth to the town. Dust blows down Main Street and rises to blot out the view of the nearby Sierra.

As early as 1868 an observer warned Californians that their children and grandchildren would pay for their reckless withdrawals from what time had stored: "Poverty as hopeless as that of the Sahara must inevitably overtake a country that is thus willfully given over to vandal cultivation." Poverty would, in turn, corrupt the society built upon it. "Of what use will be good govern-ment to a country which has been desolated by cultivators of the soil who have raised matricidal hands against our common mother earth?"[12]

Frank Norris set his turn-of-the-century novel, *The Octopus*, in the neighborhood of Pixley. He, too, linked violence toward land to that of society, and to poverty. Beneath his epic tale of conflict between farmers and the railroad, he found a fundamental attitude toward land that he called "the true California spirit," an attitude that dated to the Gold Rush and never died:

"One Tree," mural by Rigo, San Francisco, 1996

They had no love for their land. They were not attached to the soil. They worked their ranches as a quarter of a century before, they had worked their mines. To husband the resources of their marvelous San Joaquin, they considered niggardly, petty, Hebraic. To get all there was out of the land, to squeeze it dry, to exhaust it, seemed their policy. When at last, the land worn out, would refuse to yield, they would invest their money in something else; by then, they would all have made fortunes. They did not care. "After us, the deluge."[13]

Those who made their fortunes in the San Joaquin and in the state's boom towns now gone bust have gone elsewhere and don't know

its towns. For those in Pixley and Pittsburg, in the drug-ravaged towns of Hanford, East Los Angeles, Oildale, Richmond, El Centro, and Eureka, and in the dozens of penitentiaries rising throughout the Golden State, the deluge has come. For those others of Totowa or Saahatpa or Nomi Lackee, as for the uncounted birds and salmon with which they lived, it came long ago, driving them into unwhispering silence forever. Into that silence, too, went the California grizzly bear, adopted as the symbol of the state, and honored on its flag.

Let us look then at the absence of things, that we may better weigh the value of what we have gained by their loss.

Logging

Results of fire, salvage logging, flood, and massive landslide that closed Highway 50, near Whitehall, 1997

Aerial view of clear-cut logging on federal lands traded to lumber companies to create Redwood National Park, North Coast, 1992

Pieces of whalebone dried in yard, San Francisco, c. 1890 (courtesy San Francisco Maritime NHP, A12.232 pl.)

"Clearcutting Kills Salmon" sign, Half Moon Bay, 1992

Beaver pelt, Sutter's Fort, Sacramento, 1995

Dead coyote on barbed wire fence, near Copperopolis, 1994

Stack of antlers and locomotive, Alturas, 1995

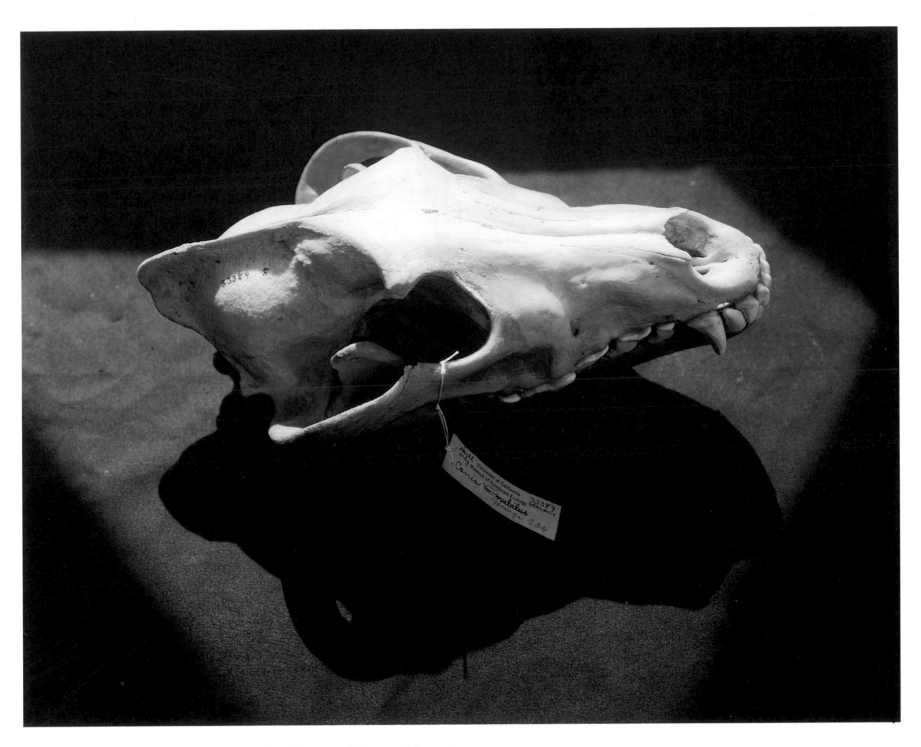

Extinct California wolf specimen, Museum of Vertebrate Zoology, University of California, Berkeley, 1996

Large-scale riverbed excavations, Feather River, 1891 (photo by Carleton Watkins, courtesy Bancroft Library)

TWO: THE PRICE OF GOLD

If there is a holy place on the Pacific Coast, it is not Father Serra's tomb at the Carmel Mission but Coloma on the American River. There you can find the taproot of Californians' materialism, as well as of the mayhem they have long inflicted on their land and on one another.

As every California school child once knew, James Marshall plucked a nugget from the tailrace of Sutter's Mill at Coloma on January 24, 1848. In doing so, Marshall kicked off the Gold Rush that led to California's admission to the Union less than three years later. His accidental find, far more than the efforts of friars given to hair shirts and self-renunciation, set the tone for the state that has long called itself golden.

Never mind that the United States was well aware that California had gold before it declared war on Mexico in 1846, or that squatters forced Sutter and Marshall off the lands they claimed and swindled them out of all that they owned. Failure to profit from his discovery and fame made Marshall a depressed and embittered drunk, preventing full canonization until death silenced his complaints in 1885. Five years later, the Native Sons of the Golden West raised a monument over his grave. From a hilltop above the town, a larger-than-life statue of Marshall points to the site on the American River where he found the fateful nugget. The state has made it a park and erected a replica of John Sutter's mill as a shrine to the memory of its two dispossessed heroes.

Fifty years after the Gold Rush, Marshall and the events he set in motion had become essential to California's legend. Poems, songs, novels, and newspapers endlessly repeated the "romance of mining," a romance that increasingly and deliberately obscured reality for the sake of those who sought to open fresh fields for the industry. Marshall was made the state's Romulus, and the aging Argonauts of 'Forty-Nine—self-organized into hereditary pioneer societies—marched through sham triumphal arches to celebrate the golden anniversary of the epochal event. Those who questioned the legend were denounced for impiety.

Many did so nonetheless, and right from the start. Ministers, tourists, and scientists questioned the hysteria that gold excited in otherwise decent men and women, as well as the effects that it had on land and society. "The people are running over the country and

Iron Mountain Mine
Clear Lake
Sacramento R.
Feather R.
Yuba R.
American R.
Malakoff Diggins/
North Bloomfield
Comstock Lode/
Virginia City
Lake Tahoe
Coloma
Penn Mine
San Jose
New Almaden mines
N
Randsburg
Mother Lode
0   50   100   150 miles

Mining Sites

picking [gold] out of the earth, just as a thousand hogs let loose in a forest would root up the ground nuts," wrote the Reverend Walter Colton of Monterey as the Gold Rush got under way.[1] Henry David Thoreau called the Gold Rush "the greatest disgrace to mankind" since it encouraged the wildest kind of speculation, and transience rather than the patience necessary for lasting settlement. Others described the miners as locusts, vultures, or savages as they stripped the surface gold from the streams of the Sierra and the soil from its hills. They jumped claims, turned on one another with a lawlessness soon celebrated as mythic Western manliness, and died of dysentery, drunkenness, loneliness, and cold. They ran the despised Mexicans and Chinese out of town, then abandoned those same towns to follow rumors of richer color over the hills. They torched the forests and the chaparral to reveal more gold among the ashes. The world's greatest stag party became California, which was trashed in the process as thoroughly as a saloon in a drunken brawl.

One journalist observed in 1873 that on the way to Yosemite "every foot almost of the soil, for mile after mile, has been at some time turned over by the gold seekers. River beds were laid bare. . . . The earth all the way to the foot-hills was removed."[2] Throughout the Sierra foothills, the physical evidence of the Gold Rush remains as piles of rock and sinuous ditches diverting water to wherever it was needed. The boulder-strewn wreckage of human frenzy surrounds picturesque Mother Lode towns strung along Highway 49, and the sites of others that have vanished. Trees and grass root in the old rubble, giving it the look of ancient ruins and contributing to the comforting illusion that nature heals all.

Less picturesque are the pits slashed through the Sierra foothills by hydraulic monitors. At Malakoff Diggins in Nevada County, the state maintains an idyllic mining town as a park and monument to an industry born and ultimately outlawed in California.

The town of North Bloomfield takes its name from the greatest of the hydraulic mines. Grass lawns and a drowsy quiet have replaced the twenty-four-hour din of batteries of water cannons and the roar of earth and pine trees falling into the pits around the town. Tourists inspect giant cast iron nozzles called monitors, which miners used to blast apart the hills in search of nuggets and dust buried in ancient riverbeds. Invented in 1853, hydraulic mining quickly grew into a high-tech, capital-intensive industry that required machine shops, banks, and exchanges in San Francisco, just as it did a vast network of reservoirs, flumes, and ditches in the high country. The latter gave the monitors the hydrostatic pressure they needed to do their work in the foothills.

White jets arching from giant pivoted nozzles made men geologic agents, and they exulted in their power. The pits became tourist attractions, providing tangible proof of the progress made in the nineteenth century toward the control and conquest of nature.

A growing number of observers were nonetheless horrified by the changes wrought by the monitors as they washed mountains of "overburden" into the nearest streams and rivers. The owners of North Bloomfield and of other mines cared little, however, for what happened beyond their own property lines. The gold that their mines added to the state's economy, they insisted, more than made up for whatever inconvenience they might cause to those downstream. They consistently relied upon numbers, rather than on their senses, when defending their actions in the mountains.

Others were not so sure of the cost-benefit ratio. Tourist Samuel Bowles wrote, "Tornado, flood, earthquake, and volcano combined could hardly make greater havoc, spread wider ruin and wreck, than are to be seen everywhere in the track of the larger gold-washing operations. None of the interior streams of California, though naturally pure as crystal, escape the change to a thick yellow mud."

Statue of James Marshall at Gold Discovery Site State Park, Coloma, 1995

Hydraulic mining at Malakoff Diggins, 1871 (photo by Carleton Watkins, courtesy Bancroft Library)

Moreover, the hydraulic companies were given legal precedence over anything obstructing them: "There are no rights which mining respects in California," said Bowles. "It is the one supreme interest." Miners were entitled by law to work directly through a producing farm, turning it into "the very devil's chaos."[3]

Hydraulic operations created havoc that shocked even an age of laissez-faire enterprise. Within three decades, monitors dislodged a volume of rock and soil from the Sierra estimated at eight times what was moved for the Panama Canal. The erosion they caused was augmented by logging, fires, and road- and railroad-building. Mudflows moved down the canyons, choking them with debris and filling valley riverbeds. In wet years, the tributaries of the Sacramento River rampaged across the bottomlands, rising as a turbid sea to drown the state capital. Silt-laden floods wrecked towns, buried farms and ranches, and destroyed inland navigation, while San Francisco Bay grew progressively muddier and more shallow as shoals appeared and marshes spread around its margins. Ships approaching San Francisco in the spring encountered the pulverized Sierra as a coffee-colored stain fanning from the Golden Gate.

Unable to ignore so much evidence of ruin to other people's property, federal judge Lorenzo Sawyer stunned the advocates of unrestrained free enterprise by ordering the North Bloomfield mine to cease operations on January 7, 1884. His decision set the precedent needed to gradually shut down other hydraulic mines. The damage, however, had been done; the mines were a gift to a few that kept on taking from all, and especially from posterity.

From the ground, the Malakoff badlands are nearly as impressive as when photographer Carleton Watkins photographed them in operation, though trees are gradually obscuring views of the vermilion bluffs ringing the amphitheaters. From the air, however, the pits retain their wild grandeur, linking together into a long wound gashed through the foothills. Well over a century after they ceased operations, the mines continue to bleed "slickens" into rivers, which are rapidly filling reservoirs and choking hydroelectric penstocks. The public cost of the diggings quickly loses its romance for anyone moving downstream with a bent for long-term accounting.

The state has erected dams to hold back the worst of the debris from the hydraulic mines, but the nation's taxpayers have had to bear most of the cost. As early as 1888 a leading San Francisco magazine insisted that since the federal government had permitted hydraulic mining to destroy the state's navigable waterways in the first place by selling public lands to the miners, "it appears but an act of justice that liberal appropriations should be made to repair the injury."[4] Congress accordingly tapped the Treasury to correct what Californians had so eagerly done to themselves.

Farther downstream, the Army Corps of Engineers has built colossal levees to protect lives and property in Marysville, Yuba City, and other towns. Farther still, at even greater public expense, the Corps has added flood-control basins to its immense levee systems to protect Sacramento and its sprawling suburbs. Its dredging operations will have to continue in perpetuity as the destabilized mountains continue to move down to the sea.

Sawyer's decision did not actually end the destruction caused by hydraulicking. Barred from the Central Valley, the industry shifted to the Trinity and Klamath Rivers on the northern coast, where the Indians and fishermen who relied on the salmon runs had less clout. California engineers took the industry with them to Oregon, Idaho, and other western states, as well as offshore, where hydraulic mining continues to this day in countries untroubled by environmental constraints. Meanwhile, mining interests persistently tried to revive these practices in California, forever invoking the lost romance of mining and the lost profits of buried gold.

Mining debris photo used in the North Bloomfield case, 1882
(photo by J. A. Todd, courtesy California Historical Society, FN-29930)

Aerial view of gold dredging and tailings near Merced, 1986

By the turn of the century, gold dredges working the bottom-lands of the Central Valley had replaced hydraulic monitors. Mechanical behemoths featuring chain-driven buckets, they churned the alluvium of the Sierra tributaries to depths of one hundred feet and more. Using mercury to trap gold dust and nuggets, they left behind sterile windrows of river cobbles stripped of topsoil. The dredge fields make dramatic deserts east of Sacramento and along the Yuba and Feather Rivers, where their gray sterility contrasts sharply with the orchards and fields of farmers who did not sell out to the mining companies. The dredges themselves stand marooned and rusting in the midst of the mercury-tainted wastelands they made, abandoned there by the San Francisco- and London-based companies that unleashed them upon the land.

Hardrock mining, too, contributed to problems only recently faced. In the hills south of San Jose, the abandoned New Almaden mines continue to bleed mercury into the streams of Silicon Valley and San Francisco Bay. Once the second-largest quicksilver mines in the world, they supplied the metal necessary for amalgamating

Warning sign, Almaden Quicksilver County Park, San Jose, 1996

Opposite: *Vegetation killed by toxic fumes, New Almaden mines and refinery, near San Jose, 1863 (photo by Carleton Watkins, courtesy Huntington Library, San Marino, California)*

gold and silver from the ores of the West. Fumes from the New Almaden refinery sickened and killed plants, animals, and people within its narrow valley. Though mercury's dangers were well known at the time, the mining companies nonetheless dumped its roasted cinnabar into creeks that supplied San Jose with drinking water. Mercury profits built some of the loveliest estates on the San Francisco peninsula and around Boston, but the tailings left the streams of today's Silicon Valley permanently poisoned. Signs warn fishermen against eating anything from the creeks; San Francisco Bay and its aquatic inhabitants are notably rich in the metallic neurotoxin.

New Almaden is only the largest of many mercury mines abandoned throughout California. Everywhere, those and other mines continue to leach heavy metals and acids into the state's drinking and irrigation waters, a legacy to posterity usually overlooked in the tales of vast fortunes wrested from the hills and of dynasties launched by the bonanzas of the West.

I admit to a perverse fascination with old mining sites. Geologic junkyards of eroded spoils and rusted machinery cupping pools of water brilliantly tinted with acid runoff, they are among the most colorful of humanity's assaults upon the earth. As a frustrated geologist, I see in them something akin to the aftermath of volcanic eruptions; but unlike volcanoes, they destroy, rather than make, topsoil. Regions of Greece, Cyprus, and Spain mined in classical times remain wastelands thousands of years later, and I now see the same happening to my own land, with little learned from the past. Moreover, mining provided a model that other industries have followed.

We found a particularly good specimen down a dirt road in Calaveras County, where technicians were struggling to keep acids and metals from the old Penn Mine out of the Mokelumne River. Someone had scrawled "Penn Mine Toxic Pits" on a shed with a

Pomo Indian in front of toxic mine tailings,
Clear Lake, 1989

skull and crossbones near the turnoff. The owners of the mine are long gone, leaving the utility district that supplies the East Bay with its water holding the toxic bag.

Penn was a piker in comparison with Iron Mountain, a marzipan-hued deposit of copper, gold, iron, zinc, and cadmium in the Siskiyou mountains southwest of Shasta Dam. Near the peak of its production, in 1899, the *San Francisco Chronicle* described the "dreary death" the mine's smelter spread over the surrounding countryside:

"Sulfurous fumes belched from tall chimneys form a thin cloud that hangs ominously in midair as a pall that would hide from the sun the desolation, the naked hillsides, and the miserably blighted and blackened and shriveled leafless bushes and scrub pine that were once part of the fresh green hillside-carpeting." Molten slag polluted the water, which "flows back into the river, laden with chemicals that in time must certainly destroy the marine life of the Sacramento."[5]

Erosion from smelter now covered by Lake Shasta, 1941 (photo by Russell Lee for the Farm Security Administration, courtesy Library of Congress)

An EPA spokesman today describes the abandoned mine as "a machine in the bowels of the mountain that can't be turned off."[6] Rated by the EPA's Superfund toxic cleanup program as one of the ten worst sites in the nation, Iron Mountain's acidic runoff feeds a blood-red reservoir that frequently spills over into the Sacramento River, killing what fish remain there while adding kick to the drinking water of millions of Californians downstream. It is only one of countless mines that continue to bleed without cease throughout the West—"countless" because a geologist officially charged with developing an inventory of abandoned mines for the California Water Quality Control Board was given no funding by the state to do so.[7]

The toxic legacy of mining extends far beyond the hydraulic amphitheaters, dredge fields, and mineheads, for mining requires support industries, which left their own contributions to the growing costs of cleanup. San Francisco's South of Market and North Beach

Aerial view of Iron Mountain dam leaching into the
Sacramento River, near Anderson, 1992

districts lie atop soil heavily contaminated by the refineries and machine shops once clustered there, while the East Bay abounds in the former sites of explosives and chemical plants, iron works, and smelters that long used the bay as a handy dump for their wastes. Lawsuits to determine liability have increasingly consumed the Superfund's budget; cleanup, when it is done at all, primarily shifts costs to the taxpayer.

In many cases, however, cleanup is impossible, and no amount of remediation can correct the damage. Navajos and Sioux who mined the uranium needed for California reactors and weapons were never told of their sacrificial role in national security and energy policy. In most cases, soil stripped and destroyed, and all that it supported, cannot be replaced. Mining set in motion an avalanche of enduring consequences that continue to this day. It contributed far more than most realize to the absence of things once common in California.

Just as harmful as the physical damage it wrought upon the land, I believe, is the way that mining made attitudes once thought shameful appear so normal that they were quickly taken for granted and

Cyanide tanks, Queen Esther Company, Mojave District, 1907 (courtesy Huntington Library, San Marino, California)

even celebrated. Chief among these was an all-consuming material-ism with which Californians became as identified as oil-rich Texans were later. "Money is our only stimulus and the getting of it our only pleasure," boasted one miner. "Never was any country so well calculated to cultivate the spirit of avarice." [8]

Mining made the West synonymous with a get-rich-quick, gut-and-cut attitude. Gambling, especially with other people's money, pervaded nearly every aspect of life, fueled by the illusion that all could achieve the well-advertised successes of the few. The scandals of a later era whose president closely identified with the Hollywood westerns in which he had starred suggest that little has changed but the dimensions of the costs passed on to the public and to posterity.

I remain fascinated by the legacy of mining, whether standing on an old tailings pile in a lonely valley or viewing historical images in the archives. Above all, when I look at Carleton Watkins's pho-tographs of the Tahoe Basin flayed of its pines, of the hydraulic can-nons laying waste to the Sierra foothills and gold dredges to the Central Valley, when I see pictures of smelters belching and ore skips

dumping their smoking slag into salmon runs and drinking water, or smoke from the strip-mined coal seams of Four Corners hanging low in the Grand Canyon, or clouds of uranium oxide dust blowing off the dumps in the Southwest, I know that the most enduring legacy of the California Gold Rush has been its unreflective violence. If the miners could do that to a place they so frequently claimed to love, then they could do it to one another—and they did.

Glamorized by Hollywood and television, the mayhem of the mining camps entered the national bloodstream like the runoff from the mines staining the rivers. Not even farming was immune, for in California, agriculture became something else altogether.

Above: *Monument to terminus of 20-Mule Team Borax and KFC, Mojave, 1995*

Opposite: *Yellow Aster Saloon, Randsburg, interior bar and gaming table (courtesy Huntington Library, San Marino, California)*

Large corporate farm, near Bakersfield, 1983

THREE: COERCED CORNUCOPIA

Imagine a feudal system endowed with space-age technology piped and wired to a planetary grid and you might picture the Westlands. While adding its tonnage of crops to the total which makes California one of the premier farming regions of the world, the Westlands resembles nothing like a Grant Wood or Norman Rockwell image of a farm. Its laser-leveled baronies of tomatoes and cotton stretch to the horizon, sparsely punctuated by managerial manor houses, its fields worked by gigantic combines. Many of the lords of these dominions work from boardrooms in distant cities while their serfs toil under fierce sun and a rain of chemicals. So mechanized has production become in the Westlands that service towns such as Mendota and Huron are few in number and have some of the highest rates of poverty—with all attendant social problems—found in the state. The landscape resembles farming about as much as a Ford assembly plant resembles a crofter's cottage. That is why agriculture is called California's leading *industry,* and why we commonly strip it of the suffix "culture" and dub it agribusiness. The California version of farming has, for nearly a century, been changing the production of food here and around the world, just as it began by changing the soil after the Gold Rush into something else altogether.

Explorers of early California recounted grasses rising higher than a man on horseback. Valley oaks reached astonishing size, and the state's conifers, too, seemed afflicted with gigantism. They did so at least partly because water tables were high then, and because their roots drew upon a reservoir of solar energy banked over countless generations to which they, in time, added their own organic substance. The valley soils of California formed a humus-rich skin as fertile as those of the Mediterranean once were. Here was a new world for the taking; the size of the native vegetation suggested fortunes to the men who claimed the land first, and who forced it to yield to the cow and the plow.

Frank Norris was hardly alone in likening California's farms to mines. The analogy was common among those who observed the new state. After all, the miners' ethos extended to every other aspect of the environment: sequoias, wildlife, whales, fish, people, oil, and

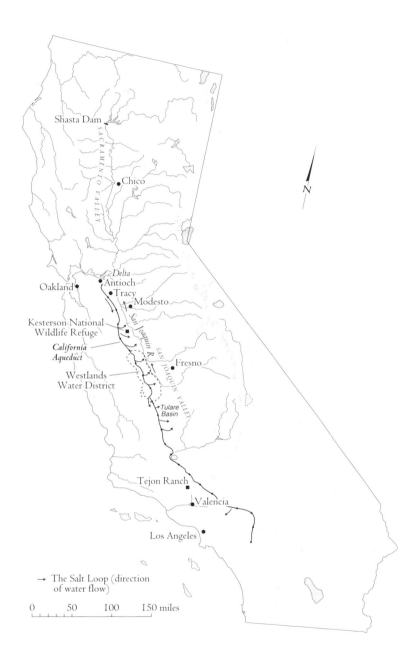

Shasta Dam

SACRAMENTO VALLEY

Chico

Delta
Antioch
Oakland
Tracy
Modesto

Kesterson National
Wildlife Refuge

San Joaquin R.

*California
Aqueduct*

SAN JOAQUIN VALLEY

Westlands
Water District

Fresno

Tulare
Basin

Tejon Ranch

Valencia

Los Angeles

→ The Salt Loop (direction
of water flow)

0   50   100   150 miles

An Altered Waterscape

water all became lucrative ore on the city's markets. Soil was no exception, for in the marketplace, it ceased to be a living thing and became, instead, paper.

Broken to the plow, the soils briefly poured their stored energy into monster vegetables and fruits and bonanza wheat yields. For the first few years, crops of forty to fifty bushels of wheat per acre were not uncommon. The strain of steady extraction quickly showed itself in a drastic dropoff to ten or twelve bushels, but that was seldom the concern of the ranchers. Of those men Norris concluded, "When at last, the land worn out, would refuse to yield, they would invest their money in something else; by then, they would all have made fortunes. They did not care."[1]

"The true California spirit," as he called it, expressed itself, again, in disposable towns resembling grim mining camps and in floating armies of impoverished migrant laborers. In a description of the bleak prospect of a typical wheat farm, the *Sacramento Daily Union* in 1870 drew the link between exploitative farming and the rural poverty that it produced. The newspaper predicted, "We see nothing in prospect but a shiftless drifting backward further and further into barbarism, until, the fertility of the soil being exhausted, the reckless and half-civilized tillers of it shall be compelled to migrate."[2] Even the heartily promotional Charles Nordhoff found the farms dreary and ephemeral. A farmer he reproached for doing nothing to beautify his property replied, "We don't go a cent on any thing but wheat in this county; we all want to get rich in two years." They would then, like the miners, move on.[3]

California was not what the Founding Fathers envisioned. Thomas Jefferson's hope for a democratic nation built on the labor of small farmers broke upon the rocky spine of the Sierra Nevada. In the new world between the mountains and the sea, circumstances

Old California ranch, Del Puerto Canyon, 1995

Factory in the fields: large chicken farm in the San Joaquin Valley, 1989

Opposite: *Cracked mud and vineyard, near Arvin, 1985*

Field of cotton about to be harvested, near Five Points, 1985

created the conditions for a quite different society, one more resembling the Old World or the Old South. Lax laws, corruption, and epic fraud combined with vast Mexican land grants and an arid climate to produce a world-renowned degree of land monopoly that shapes the landscape to this day.[4] A few men locked up the best lands in immense hereditary estates whose owners built their wooden Victorian palaces overlooking San Francisco and whose descendants move through today's society columns. By the early 1870s, a mere half of 1 percent of California's population owned half of the privately held land in the state.[5] *Sunset* magazine observed that "not

even Old England provided a finer example of baronial and ducal landlords than the Great Valley of California."[6] Commenting on "a phenomenon rare in the United States," an English tourist noted, "The land system of California presents features both peculiar and dangerous, a contrast between great properties, often appearing to conflict with the general weal, and the sometimes hard pressed small farmer, together with a mass of unsettled labour, thrown without work into the towns at certain times of the year."[7]

Principalities of such an extent are themselves essential to the legend of western opportunity, satisfying a general yearning for the

Scientist and dead chickens (courtesy Del Monte Collection, Oakland Museum of California)

royalty that Americans lost in 1776. They form the basic props of popular television sagas such as *Bonanza, Napa,* and the Carol Burnett spoof of same, *Fresno.* An official history of the Tejon Ranch by a member of the family that owned it lyrically plays upon that desire for dynastic glory buttressed with historical precedent: "The aboriginal Indians, the Spaniards, the Mexicans, and the Americans ruling the empire at various times had one common bond. They all loved land—wild, unsettled land—as far as the human eye can see and the red orbs of the mighty condor can encompass in a day's leisurely flight."[8] No television series has ever followed the lives of the far more numerous roustabouts barred from ownership by such voracious love of the land; John Steinbeck is still regarded by some as a communist for doing so in *The Grapes of Wrath.*

The fiefdoms of the Central Valley demanded ever more sophisticated technology and growing amounts of energy to extract maximum returns with a minimum of skilled labor. Absentee landowners such as Haggin & Tevis, Chandler, Miller & Lux, and Hearst had the means and the machines to extract those profits from their ranches in the provinces. California's foundries produced the latest in customized reapers, seeders, and gang plows for the vast fields.

Entrance to a large farm, near Grimes, 1984

Centrifugal pumps allowed ranchers to mine water at greater depth, clamshell dredges made it possible to dike and dry out marshlands, and ditchers helped them excavate irrigation canals. Stockton's Holt Caterpillar Company developed a continuous-tread tractor so ideally suited to soggy soils that the British adapted it for military tanks and transports in World War I. Mechanical tomato harvesters required genetically altered fruit with an armored skin and the texture of styrofoam, and these the state university laboratories provided. Machine shops in the valley towns continue to produce ingenious customized farming equipment, while biotechnology engineers the crops.

Small wonder that the valley's famous artesian wells went dry in twenty years from overdraft. Water tables sank, along with the land, and springs dried up. No longer able to reach moisture, trees, grass, and bushes died and much of the San Joaquin's soil, broken to the plow, turned to dust in the age-old process known as desertification. Rain furrowed the plowed and overgrazed fields with erosion channels or peeled it off in sheets and sent it down the rivers to the sea. Herds of livestock grazed forage to the roots while pounding it to the consistency of concrete. During the hearings on the effects of hydraulic mining, General John Bidwell of Chico told Judge Lorenzo Sawyer's court that millions of hoofs had made the valley lands "harder" than they had been when he pioneered the northern Sacramento Valley. Rain ran off it rather than settling in.

Nonetheless, the land continued to yield a phenomenal bounty whose much-boasted value, like that of mining, obscured social and environmental costs that grew as the shadow to California's legendary abundance. Wheat gave way in time to a dazzling array of crops ranging from fruits and nuts—prunes, almonds, peaches, olives, walnuts, grapes, and apples in the north, and citrus and avocados in the south—to fresh vegetables, oil seeds, alfalfa, rice, tomatoes, flowers, and cotton. Animals, too, continue to be an important sector of agribusiness, their lives adapted and their genes altered, like tomatoes, to assembly-line production. Some regions became world famous for their glamour products: the Santa Clara Valley for its prunes and apricots, Los Angeles for oranges, and Napa for its wine grapes. Farmers and land companies experimented incessantly. In 1871 a railroad promotional magazine opined, "There is probably no crop which offers to the capitalist so profitable a return for the money invested as does that of Opium." The *Mining and Scientific Press* likewise touted opium as "just the crop to afford employment for families where there are large numbers of children too young for field hands."[9]

Human ingenuity and capital turned California into the greatest food and fiber factory the world has ever known. By 1905, long before the term "Green Revolution" was coined to refer to the means of feeding exploding populations, a headline in the *San Francisco Chronicle* boasted, "California's Method of Agriculture Now a Model for the World."[10] Like a factory, agribusiness needed an assured input of energy and water, and these, too, the creativity of its inventors and engineers provided.

The first half-century of California farming was marked by a free-for-all of drilling, ditching, and diverting to move water from where it was ostensibly wasted to where it would produce a secure and high rate of return on arid soil. In the 1880s, the San Francisco–based firms of Haggin & Tevis and Miller & Lux locked legal horns over who "owned" the surface waters in the southern San Joaquin Valley. The landmark case of *Lux v. Haggin* produced an indecisive result known as the California Doctrine of water appropriation, which guaranteed that those law firms specializing in the arcane nuances

Deep stream erosion, San Lorenzo Creek, Peachtree Valley (diptych), 1995

Opposite: *Terraces made by cattle, near Westley, 1984*

Workers in a packing plant (courtesy California Historical Society, FN-30648)

Aerial view of rice field, Sacramento Valley, 1986

Wagonload of prunes, Visalia (courtesy Geography Department, University of California, Berkeley)

Opposite: *Harvest truck, near Lodi, 1985*

of water law would rank among the wealthiest and most powerful in the nation.[11] No other course was possible in a land of finite water supplies where competing demands were accelerating toward infinity.

The tendency toward land and water concentration did not go unchallenged. Using California as his model, self-made economist Henry George argued in clear and passionate language that land monopoly historically lay at the heart of all undemocratic societies, producing widespread poverty with a few pinnacles of dazzling wealth. His 1879 book *Progress and Poverty* became an international best-seller, inciting many to call for a breakup and distribution of the great estates. A powerful grangers' movement spoke for the small grower; in 1887, it persuaded the California legislature to permit farmers to form cooperative irrigation districts as a means of opposing the power of the land barons.

Nonetheless, the costs of moving water grew prohibitive even to large ranchers and growers, particularly when the automatic flow of artesian wells fell off as abruptly as the productivity of the soil. Only communal action on a formerly unthinkable scale, combined with virtually unlimited energy, could bring a maximum amount of "wasteland" into productive use.

Congress in 1902 passed the Reclamation Act, committing the federal government to building dams and moving rivers to wherever they could best be used. Those who opposed the tendency toward land monopoly insisted that the act contain an unmistakable rule that publicly subsidized waters would go to farms no larger than 160 acres, and that those farms *must* be owner-occupied. The 160-acre limitation and residency requirement were designed to frustrate absentee land speculators. Though worded in terms far clearer than the California Doctrine, those twin provisions would provide another fertile field of sophistry for attorneys employed by the land

barons. The Reclamation Act said nothing about urban real estate.

Its passage coincided with the birth of California's energy grid. As entrepreneurs tapped the force of falling water and brought in gushers of petroleum, the price of power dropped precipitously. Energy appeared miraculously wherever the wires, pipes, and tanker cars carried it. By 1915, *Sunset* magazine could boast that the San Joaquin Valley produced 25 percent of the nation's petroleum, and that cheap oil combined with the internal combustion engine and the electric pump had lowered the cost of agricultural pumping by 40 percent. Further gains in production, it said, could be made if the state built irrigation projects—even if that meant that the government would have to be given some say in how much land an individual or corporation could farm.[12]

Any such restriction, however, represented for many large growers an intolerable violation of individual liberties. Historian Bernard DeVoto once succinctly defined the western attitude to the federal government as "Get out and give us more money."[13]

For a few decades, the tendency toward concentration appeared to reverse. The heirs of some of the passing cattle and wheat barons sought to liquidate their assets, and the Southern Pacific, with land grants of more than 11 million acres, wanted carrier revenues, which a well-settled state would provide. Rising labor costs and taxes, and declining soil fertility, made the breakups even more attractive, as did the value added by electric interurban trains and irrigation canals. A national magazine in 1909 described a near-unanimous passion to attract more people to California and the promotion designed to achieve that end: "To deal adequately with nature at wholesale," said *The World's Work,* "the state needs more men. The land needs farmers to help them grasp the great opportunities requiring common support; the cities need markets; the country needs cities. The process works in a circle, and to the advantage of all concerned, for the new settler profits by the better land and better methods he finds when he settles. So the task of attracting new people is undertaken by all." [14]

Agricultural colonies sprang up or were projected the length of the state at the same time that older farming towns were reinvigorated by an influx of new settlers. The town of Modesto erected a triumphal arch in 1911 near the train station that announced, in electric letters, "WATER, WEALTH, CONTENTMENT, HEALTH." *Sunset* boasted that the town had "no whittling loafers, only busy drummers," and "neat bungalows by the hundred." [15] A growing network of electric interurbans, and of rural telephones and mail delivery, promised to end the traditional isolation of the farm and to speed produce to cities; the 180-mile Sacramento Northern Railroad reaching from Oakland to Chico was the longest interurban in the nation, providing a spinal column from which branch lines began to reach out to farming towns throughout the Sacramento Valley. To celebrate the subdivision of the great ranchos, the *San Francisco Chronicle* sponsored a Land Show in October 1913. A half-page illustration showed the goddess Fortuna striding across a prosperous California. It was headlined "Forward to the Land." [16]

We can only wonder what the state might have been had that vision of resettlement been realized. The electric interurban came too late, however, for the automobile and the truck quickly wiped it out. The Depression reversed the breakup of the land baronies, throwing thousands of California farmers off the land and adding hundreds of thousands of landless immigrants from the midwestern Dust Bowl and the South to a desperate labor pool. Dorothea Lange's photograph of a Kern County service station with the crudely lettered sign "AIR — THIS IS YOUR COUNTRY — DON'T LET THE BIG MEN TAKE IT AWAY FROM YOU," contradicted the upbeat message on the Modesto arch and summarized the bitterness that attended

Beginning of agriculture, Pasadena, c. 1880 (photo by Carleton Watkins, courtesy Huntington Library, San Marino, California)

Construction of Shasta Dam, 1941 (photo by Russell Lee for the Farm Security Administration, courtesy Library of Congress)

an epidemic of farm foreclosures. By 1936 the Bank of America's holding company, Transamerica, had alone acquired 2,642 farms totaling more than a half-million acres, more even than claimed by the giant Kern County Land Company in California.[17]

Government aided the creation of new baronies in programs designed, or advertised, to do just the opposite. In 1944 the Bureau of Reclamation closed the outlet gates on its massive new Shasta Dam, creating a gigantic reservoir at the head of the Sacramento Valley as the northern linchpin of its Central Valley Project (CVP), the largest of all its schemes. Designed to store floodwaters, generate electricity, and move water at public expense from the relatively wet Sacramento Valley to the San Joaquin Valley, the CVP gave instant value to desert lands far to the south. Agribusiness in fact would scarcely exist without such stupendous public assistance. Through legal legerdemain and a compliant Bureau of Reclamation, individuals and corporations persistently evaded both acreage limitation and residency requirements while applying heavily subsidized water to holdings of up to tens of thousands of acres.[18] Economies of scale, spokesmen for agribusiness persistently argued, simply made the small farm obsolete.

Yet there remained, firmly embedded in the very act that gave birth to the Bureau of Reclamation, that explicit clause designed to spread the benefits of public subsidies among the maximum number of resident farmers.

Few might have noticed but for an economist at the University of California whom one historian has called "the last Jeffersonian."[19] Coming from a Wisconsin farming family, Paul Taylor was shocked by the disparity of wealth he found in California, which he, like Henry George, traced to land monopoly. In a series of elegantly concise legal briefs and articles, Professor Taylor fought a long and often lonely battle to make the government enforce its own law.

Largely because of Taylor, the 160-acre limitation remained a burr under the saddle of federally subsidized irrigation, threatening to unseat agribusiness and continuing to cost it much in legal and lobbying fees. If it could not free itself of that irritant on the national level, then it could find other ways to maintain the status quo.

In 1960, in league with southern California land developers and with the help of sophisticated public relations, the industry persuaded California voters to pay for the greatest of all water-moving schemes, the State Water Project. The SWP was designed to dam the Feather River and send it down the San Joaquin Valley, via the California Aqueduct, to southern California cities. Working in tandem, the SWP and the CVP created a hydraulic shell game incomprehensible to most outsiders, while the deliberate omission of acreage limitations in the State Water Project breathed new life into the fiefdoms owned by major oil, chemical, and insurance companies, especially in the Westlands Water District. The farmers of the Westlands had names like Standard Oil and Southern Pacific, which gave the district immense political clout in Sacramento and Washington. The names of other farmers were hidden in a maze of corporate dummies. Unfortunately, all growers had problems when they applied taxpayer-financed water to the dry alluvial ramp along the west side of the San Joaquin.

Underlain by shallow layers of clay, the Westlands soils quickly became waterlogged when irrigated. They also contained salt and alkali left from past ages when the valley was flooded by an inland arm of the sea, including something that made cattlemen avoid the area and geologists recommend against farming it. The soil was bad,

San Leandro Oyster Beds Monument, San Leandro, 1995

they said. Cows went blind, staggered, and collapsed after eating the forage that grew on it. The answer, according to the state, the Bureau of Reclamation and their clients, was to connect the "service areas" with a half-billion dollar master drain running down the center of the valley. The drain would dump toxic agricultural sewage into the sea, which agribusiness spokesmen defined as reaching as far inland as Antioch on the San Joaquin Delta. Antioch in fact sat thirty-five miles east of the Golden Gate and only a few miles downstream from the intake for the federal and state pumps. Those pumps sucked ostensibly fresh water from the Delta, sending it back to the San Joaquin ranches and on to southern California cities, which used it for drinking water.

Cost and environmental objections stopped the master drain ninety miles shy of its goal. There, in the marshes near Los Banos, wastewater ponded and concentrated in the grasslands once grazed by Miller & Lux cattle, providing food for a dwindling number of waterfowl traveling the Pacific Flyway. Within the grasslands, too, was Kesterson National Wildlife Refuge. Reclamation officials claimed that Kesterson could use agricultural runoff to support waterfowl and the duck clubs who shot them for sport. Unfortunately, the birds hatched there didn't look right to neighbors and biologists.

Ranchers bordering the refuge reported foul odors and sick cattle. United States Fish and Wildlife scientists found extremely high levels of dead bird embryos in the marshes and chicks with grotesque birth defects. They identified the problem as selenium, a trace element occurring naturally in desert soils throughout the arid West. Irrigation waters had dissolved selenium and, like mining debris loosened by hydraulic cannons, moved it downhill. Kesterson, it seemed, was less a refuge than a toxic deathtrap whose name joined those of Love Canal and Stringfellow as a place to be avoided.

But Kesterson was only a small part of the dark backdrop to the apparent success of California agribusiness, a backdrop that increasingly and insistently moved to center stage. In the same year that it closed the gates on Shasta Dam at the head of the Sacramento River, the Bureau of Reclamation completed Friant Dam on the San Joaquin River, shunting the river in canals along the east side of the valley as far south as Bakersfield. Friant quickly dried up the San Joaquin, turning its lower course into little more than a drainage ditch for agricultural waste waters and starving the Delta and the bay of more than a fifth of their fresh water inflow. Within five years, salmon counts on the San Joaquin plunged from a high of 60,000 to zero.

None of the promotion for agribusiness mentioned that another leading food industry would have to die so that it could live and grow. San Francisco Bay, the Delta, and the rivers that fed them provided a nursery for fish and shellfish that once made the region one of the nation's leading fishing ports. The *San Francisco Bulletin* boasted, in 1904, "Pacific Coast Fisheries Feed the World," while shrimp and crab taken from the bay made Fisherman's Wharf one of the city's leading tourist attractions. The mighty salmon runs that streamed through Carquinez Strait and up the rivers of the Central Valley fed canneries and provided work for thousands in the Bay Area.

Frank Quan, the last of the fishermen at Marin's China Camp, noticed the change when Friant Dam choked the San Joaquin. "It was so gradual that at first we didn't realize the effect of the diversion," he told a reporter in 1992. "Now we are at about bottom today. There is no flounder out there, the bass are about gone and the shrimp are about gone too, unless we get some heavy rain." Agribusiness may have been correct about the Pacific reaching as far inland as Antioch, because its extractions had simply moved the ocean:

Aerial view of soil salinization, San Joaquin Valley, 1991

"There is not enough water getting into the Bay," lamented Quan, "and now all the Bay water is as salty as the sea. . . . The fishermen all quit and moved away from the camp because there were no fish."[20] By the 1990s, salmon throughout the Central Valley were nearing extinction.

Not only the bay was salting up; far to the south, alkali crusted the furrows like snow in the desert sun. From the air, the irrigated fields of the Tulare Basin looked like threadbare green carpets as salts killed the crops. In the thousands of years since it destroyed the fields of Mesopotamia's Fertile Crescent, and the cities that de-

pended on them, salt has cursed the farmer of irrigated desert lands, and California is no exception. Besides the salts that occur naturally in desert soils, imported water carries minute quantities, which make that water brinier every year because of the peculiar nature of the San Joaquin Valley's manmade plumbing.

Of the 3 million tons of salt that federal and state aqueducts annually carry into the San Joaquin Valley, some escapes down the ditch once known as the San Joaquin River. Once in the Delta, some of that drainwater is picked up by the pumps near Tracy and sent back down the aqueducts to be reapplied to the fields. Growers, too, dump directly into the federal Delta-Mendota Canal, which mixes with state water at the San Luis Forebay. Publicly financed projects have thus made the San Joaquin Valley an immense salt loop, a major outlet for which are the taps of southern California.

Salts are not the only substance accumulating in California's soils and groundwater. Agribusiness has waxed fat on chemicals that turn soil from an organic matrix into a hydroponic medium with the nutritive qualities of cardboard; indeed, the cost of fertilizers, soil fumigants, growth hormones, herbicides, defoliants, fungicides, pesticides, and systemic poisons has helped make farming prohibitively expensive and has contributed to the reconcentration of land. In 1988 growers spread a reported 34,282 tons of pesticide active ingredients on the Central Valley alone. For the traveler crossing the valley, the air smells at times like a chemical plant. Most people will quickly pass on to more desirable destinations, but those who live there, and especially those who work the fields and processing plants, have no way of avoiding it.

California's agricultural workers have long been treated as expendable, for there are always more when they are needed. Their inexhaustibility and desperation have kept wages at or below subsistence level, and the price of food in the supermarkets correspondingly reasonable. This, too, is an old tradition dating back to the land barons who ran their ranches like southern plantations or mines: when legislation checked the flood tide of imported Chinese in 1882, growers replaced them in turn with Japanese, Sikhs, Filipinos, Armenians, Italians, Portuguese, Okies, and, increasingly, with Mexicans and Central Americans. All have been despised and mistreated as outsiders by those who arrived earlier.

In the 1990s a new wave of scapegoating once again focused on immigrants from south of the border, finding in them an explanation for California's deepening economic and environmental woes.

By then, however, California agribusiness was more dependent on foreign-born workers than ever before. The California Institute for Rural Studies reported that 92 percent of workers were immigrants, and that more would be constantly needed, since grueling and dangerous working conditions encouraged few children to follow in their parents' line of work. "If we weren't here," quipped one Mexican laborer, "maybe they'd bring in some Somalis to do the work."[21]

Agribusiness, it is often said, is the means for transforming petroleum into food. It is hardly surprising, then, that some of the largest farmers are oil companies whose auxiliary branches produce field chemicals. To a degree to which few consumers are aware, cheap and plentiful food depends on cheap and plentiful fossil fuel and hydroelectricity. Energy drives water down the canals and over the mountains; it runs the machines that plant and harvest the fields, the pumps that keep them wet or dry, the processing factories that preserve and ready food and fiber for the market, and the trucks and jets that deliver those products to global markets. Moreover, energy synthesizes the fertilizers that force soil to continue yielding after its natural fertility has been exhausted.

Agribusiness also needs water, however, and that resource is likely to expire before the oil does. In 1993 the Department of Water Resources (DWR) released a sobering report showing water demand rising far faster than the available supply. It predicted, even in wet years, a chronic, growing, and manmade drought as the state's population climbs from 30 million to an estimated 49 million by the year 2020; it suggested that California's environment would continue to decline as diversions starve it of water.

For a state so long addicted to the fantasy of perpetual growth, and to the concept of soil as real estate, such a sobering analysis could not stand in the way of tradition. A few months after the DWR report and under intense pressure from real estate and construction

Energy, oil, and farming, near Bakersfield, 1990

Opposite: *Man on an ATV burning a rice field, near Grimes, 1993*

Aerial view of new homes on Central Valley farmland, Discovery Bay, 1996

lobbies, the state legislature defeated a bill requiring local governments to identify sources of water before permitting developers to build.

The DWR report may ironically have helped to spur urban growth, for developers and environmentalists were quick to point out that 85 percent of the state's captured water is devoted to farming and a mere 15 percent to cities and industries. The conclusion was obvious to some that California had, in fact, plenty of water for both growth and the environment if agriculture would simply reduce its demands. Diligent conservation measures combined with an end to government farming subsidies, claimed proponents of "water marketing," would enable growers to sell their water at a profit to thirsty cities.

Moreover, in 1982 agribusiness lobbyists finally persuaded Congress to "reform" the 1902 Reclamation Act by virtually erasing the 160-acre limitation and residency requirement, freeing the industry at last of the clause that had so long vexed it and making legal the violation of nearly eighty years' standing. Paul Taylor died eighteen months after the Reclamation Reform Act, but by then the Bureau of Reclamation was becoming less concerned with farms, either large or small, than with feeding water and energy to developers in places named Orange County, Phoenix, and Las Vegas.

Ninety years after Congress passed the Reclamation Act, twenty-one water agencies supplying more than 35 million western city dwellers formed a new lobbying group to get water from farmers. The Western Urban Water Coalition thus made a historic break in the traditional alliance between California's urban water districts and agribusiness. The former's developer-dominated boards had long made common cause with powerful growers to drive through public works such as the CVP and the SWP. By 1992, however, the West had become so citified that its voters had the clout needed to make whatever changes were necessary to produce yet more cities. The cities themselves had grown to the point that few Californians knew much about where their food came from before it appeared in supermarkets and fast-food franchises. Surely, they reasoned, it would keep coming, and be as cheap as ever.

And so, for all the bravado about the state's leading industry—about the billions of dollars that it adds to the economy and the miracles of production and technical ingenuity that it has accomplished—California's farming is on the way out, as the rising value of its soil produces more in lot sales than in cotton, cattle, or almonds. A linear city of shopping malls, housing developments, and office parks spreads along Interstate 80 from the Bay Area to Sacramento and beyond, and another along Highway 99 from Sacramento to Bakersfield on the east side of the San Joaquin. New cities of hundreds of thousands are slated for the dry west side of the San Joaquin as well, fed by Interstate 5 and the California Aqueduct and owned by some of the largest corporations and wealthiest families in California. Travelers flying between the Bay Area and Los Angeles can see them at night as webs of light coalescing on the dark plain below. Such cities will permanently bury much of the state's remaining, and best, farmlands. They will be hard pressed, however, to find water uncontaminated by salts, selenium, and chemicals left behind by the previous owners. As they grow larger, they will ensure that in a serious drought environmental guarantees will be canceled. Water going to any uses other than cities will be turned off at the dam, finishing off the last of the wildlife and the remaining orchards.

Despite the growing concentration and mechanization, many farmers remain intensely devoted to agriculture as a way of life; they want to pass it on, and they bemoan the changes coming. Of the 82,000 farms in California, 66,000, or three-fourths, produce only

Aerial view of a remnant farm surrounded by subdivisions, San Jose, 1996

The finger-posts of Romance lead along the shore of San Francisco Bay into the vale of Santa Clara where blossoming fruit orchards come down almost to the water's edge

Sunset *magazine's promotion of the Santa Clara Valley as the "Valley of Heart's Delight," March 1914*

5 percent of the state's farm products and thus classify as small. But the shift toward urbanization was made inevitable by the prevailing attitude toward soil brought by the miners. "We are not husbandmen. We are not farmers," said an agribusiness spokesman quoted by Paul Taylor in *An American Exodus*, the book on which he collaborated with his wife, Dorothea Lange, in 1939. "We are producing a product to sell."[22] The chairman of one of the last and largest family-owned baronies, the Newhall Land Company, echoed those sentiments a half-century later: "Newhall Land's legacy is not of agriculture for the sake of agriculture, but of utilizing the land as a resource," said Thomas L. Lee as his company built out Valencia and planned new cities elsewhere. "[Founder] Henry Mayo Newhall always capitalized on the land, and we are continuing in that tradition."[23]

As a child, I watched the Bay Area's Santa Clara Valley capitalized. Bulldozers uprooted the apricot and prune trees and piled them into tangled pyres that burned to embers in the night. A rigid circuitry of infrastructure glazed over the rarest soils in the world. The valley became as emblematic of Californian success and innovation as the hydraulic and mercury mines had once been. It was renamed Silicon for the chips that it makes.

In few places can one see better how high technology has uprooted urbanites from what sustains them than in Emma Prusch Park in San Jose. Toward the end of her life, says a brochure in the park, Miss Prusch deeded her cherished dairy farm to the city, "specifically request[ing] that the land keep its country feeling, preserving the quality of the Santa Clara Valley that she remembered when trees and animals were more prominent than houses, freeways, and shopping centers."

The farm formed an island in the encroaching city, which the state highway department saw as an ideal site for an interchange

Old farmhouse surrounded by freeway, Emma Prusch Park, San Jose, 1996

linking Highways 101 and 280. A futuristic ganglion of concrete took a third of the farm, barraging what remains with the thunder of traffic and exhaust from the elevated structure. The Police Activities League took another eleven acres for a ballpark. A corner has been reserved for a hundred garden plots used by those living in the nearby barrio of East San Jose, while the rest has lawns and redwood trees ideal for picnicking. In pens between Emma Prusch's prim Victorian farmhouse and a new barn built by the city, the children of Silicon Valley can see what ducks and chickens look like and pass rusted farm implements as mysterious as the relics of the Mayans. It is hard to find in that small museum what made a woman so love that place that she wished it saved for others.

Community-Supported Agriculture (CSA)

Community-supported agriculture is not-for-profit farming in which consumers and farmers work together with the common purpose of supporting agriculture that is socially and ecologically responsible. It is a new way for a farm to market its produce and finance its operation. A community buys shares at the beginning of the season, then shares equally in the farm's output as well as in the risk of a poor harvest caused by drought or pestilence. The farmer receives working capital up front and is assured of a market for all the farm's output with very little waste. In exchange, the farmer has the task of administering the program and distributing its harvest to multiple clients. Today, more than 600 CSA farms across the United States and Canada serve almost 150,000 participants.

David Visher notes in *Small Farm News* that CSAs are not just about food but also about community. The underlying premise of a CSA is that if people have a connection with the source of their food they will be willing to pay the true cost of the food, which includes supporting and building the farm as a sustainable entity.

Steve Decater of Live Power Community Farm in Covelo says, "The real cost of farming is what it takes to care for the farm in a healthy way. But people can only buy into that if it is personal enough for them to have a connection. They won't feel that shopping at Safeway. The real key is to connect production with the consumer so they can take responsibility for caring for their food. Everyone is a gardener. Everyone is eating food. In a sense they are delegating their responsibility to whomever is producing the food. If they delegate without consciousness we get into trouble. It is not just food we are producing. We are trying to recreate a conscious connection between the consumer and the producer. The marketing system creates an illusion. It blocks people from coming into a conscious connection with their food system. For people coming together in a community to take care of the environment, the food is a by-product."

Steve and his wife, Gloria, run the CSA in Covelo. Their "live power" farming makes use of existing farm life to foster more life. Very few farms today use horses to plow their fields. The Decaters do and as a result have freed their farm from depending on gasoline. Many farms can become completely reproductive and sustainable and can liberate themselves from the use of fossil energy sources. The need to produce cash crops in order to purchase energy and fertilizer outside the farm decreases. The Decaters' use of live horse power allows them to be producers rather than consumers of inputs and to create value from labor without generating crippling overhead. The farm has used horses since 1982. Steve points out that they are very efficient when you consider that they are fueled by the sun and are self-replicating. Although they are slower than tractors, they do not need nearly as many off-farm inputs as tractors. Their use is in keeping with the farm's goals of balance and self-sufficiency.

In addition to farming, Gloria and Steve conduct workshops for children and adults about stewardship of the land and sustainable agriculture. They also have an apprenticeship program, and since 1978 they have hosted fifty apprentices from all over North America and Europe, averaging seven apprentices at one time. Their long-term goal is to secure land for productive farm use into the future through community trust ownership. They are purchasing their land through a shared equity deed in which they own part of the equity and a nonprofit land trust owns the other part. With deed restrictions, the nonprofit land trust conserves the property for organic agriculture and protects it against subdivision and environmental degradation. The trust holds its part of the equity in perpetuity. The farmers may sell their part of the equity based on the agricultural potential, keeping it affordable to an incoming farmer.

We abuse the land because we regard it as a commodity belonging to us. When we see land as a community to which we belong, we may begin to use it with love and respect.

Aldo Leopold, *A Sand County Almanac*, 1949

Horse-drawn plow at Live Power Community Farm, Covelo, 1995

Oak tree restoration, Cosumnes River Preserve, 1994

*Farmer Fred Smeds working his family farm with the
American Farm Land Trust, near Reedly, 1995*

Commuter traffic flowing under Father Serra's arm, Highway 280, San Mateo County, 1997

FOUR: ENERGY'S LUMINOUS NET

The sun had yet not risen as I drove north on Highway 101 through Marin County. Traffic flowed freely in my direction, but in the other, it crawled toward San Francisco as a tightly packed stream of headlights at dawn. I imagined commuters afloat on a river of gasoline carrying them south across the Golden Gate Bridge toward the city. At the same time, major tributaries of fuel were converging from throughout the East Bay at the Bay Bridge toll plaza to form another river flowing west across that bridge, while twin streams ran in both directions on the Peninsula between San Francisco and Silicon Valley. In the valley itself, all the rivers were running together into a fuming marsh encircling San Jose. Ever-lengthening streams of liquid energy fed the Bay Area with commuters from the Central Valley as far away as the Sierra foothills. As the sun rose over the San Bernardino, San Gabriel, and Santa Monica Mountains, torrents of refined petroleum poured into the cities of southern California, and still others into Sacramento and the rapidly growing cities of the Central Valley. The roads around Lake Tahoe jammed again. All these streams converged in my mind into one collective Niagara of gasoline, leaping over the brink of a precipice into a pandemonium of traffic noise and rising clouds of smog.

Yet this was only one morning's commute; in the evening, the streams would reverse, and every year into the foreseeable future, that imaginary river would grow larger, as if, in some distant and unknown headwaters, monsoons of oil were replenishing it.

That river was not, of course, being constantly replenished. It flowed from underground reservoirs of compacted solar energy that had taken millions of years of photosynthesis to fill. The increasing size of its tributaries could only mean that the pools of oil were dropping fast, as they are. But as long as it continues to flow, that river and others directed by humans are changing the face of California nearly as dramatically as the tectonic forces that built the state's mountains and valleys. Even as it shapes the place they occupy, abundant energy also molds the thoughts and memories of the Golden State's inhabitants.

Because we now use energy so profligately, it is nearly as difficult to imagine what life would be like without it as to imagine civiliza-

Landscape where Ishi surrendered, near Oroville, 1995

tion without language. Neither one would, in fact, exist. That was a lesson brought down from the mountains by a stranger early in the century.

On August 29, 1911, a nearly naked man stumbled out of the Sierra foothills into a corral near Oroville showing severe symptoms of energy deprivation. The last of a small group of natives called the Yahi, the man had reached the end of his rope and chose to take his chances with those who had reduced him to such a state. The local sheriff locked him in the Oroville jail to protect him from crowds eager to see the freak. Within days, anthropologists from the University of California arrived to take the "wild man" to San Francisco. There, they gave him the name Ishi and lodged and fed him at the university museum while attempting to learn his language and thus his story.

Like other native inhabitants of California, the Yahi used only a trickle of the energy flowing through their environment. They took what they needed for subsistence from sunlight channeled briefly through the tissues of plants and game, leaving little room for error. The energy needs of those who came seeking gold in 1849 were far greater and quickly shrank the limits of error for others who lived so close to the present.

As they themselves were hunted and their food vanished, the rapidly dwindling Yahi retreated into hiding in the volcanic foothills of the northern Sierra. The anthropologists learned that in 1908 a surveying party scouting a remote canyon for a new hydroelectric dam had discovered their campsite. Three Indians fled at their approach, leaving an old woman too feeble to move. Having inspected the camp, the party left the woman but took nearly everything else, including food and tools, as souvenirs of their encounter. Thus robbed of both energy and the means for getting more, three of the four remaining Yahi died, and the last left the canyon in desperation.

In San Francisco, Ishi's guardians were surprised to learn that their "wild man" was little impressed by such marvels as tall buildings and airplanes. It was the crowds that stunned him, the vast throngs of people on the beaches and in the streets. The audiences in theaters fascinated him. The anthropologists took this phenomenon for granted, as did most of those whom Ishi watched in the city. Few were aware that such concentrations of people could only be sustained by drowning canyons like Ishi's hideout, and by squandering long-hoarded reserves of fossil fuels. The pipelines and wires that increasingly fed the cities distanced those city dwellers who relied on such energy from the consequences of procuring it.

Those who displaced the Yahi and other tribes after the Gold Rush were accustomed to using energy to radically alter the land, often to attract and accommodate precisely the crowds that would give that land extra value. Among their first actions, then, was to make San Francisco Bay more useful by getting rid of it.

The smell wafting off the bay was reason enough to fill it, for the by-products of the city's crowds and their appetite for energy quickly turned it into a cesspool. John Parrott, one of the city's wealthiest citizens, described in 1852 the filling of a stinking pond that had recently been the bay but was becoming the financial district: "One stands upon the edge and looks with a grim satisfaction, as load after load falls into the watery monster, every one dropping heavily, and raising a surge which restlessly moves from bank to bank." Powered by coal, an earth-moving machine called a steam paddy was doing the work of many men, making Parrott an even richer man: "We may hope soon to see stately palaces of trade rising on the site of a departed nuisance," he concluded.[1] Parrott's nuisance was the city's harbor.

For all its resources, California seemed singularly lacking in the fossil fuel necessary to stimulate industrial growth and to make

Aerial view of financial district, San Francisco, 1997

major changes in the land. Prospectors discovered seams of poor coal on Mount Diablo, thirty miles east of San Francisco, but much had to be imported at great expense from mines as far away as Australia and England. Industrialists thus had to rely on energy stored close to the present in the tissues of plants. They stripped the forests around Lake Tahoe and along the eastern Sierra to feed the furnaces of their Nevada mines; they used Chinese peasants, mules, oxen, and horses to build the railroads, drain the marshes, and accomplish other earth-moving feats.

They also used falling water. Hydraulic monitors and stream-run wheels converted the force of mountain runoff into mechanical energy at the mines, and these technologies segued neatly, at the end of the century, into hydroelectric generation and transmission.

High up a desert canyon in the San Bernardino Mountains, State Marker 514 commemorates the Pomona Water Power Plant. Here in 1892, it says, Dr. Cyrus Grandison Baldwin built California's first hydroelectric plant for the long-distance transmission of alternating current. In so doing, Baldwin succeeded not only in converting the force of water falling off the mountain into high-voltage electricity but also in moving it to where it would best produce comfort and profits. He thus launched the power grid that progressively reshapes the state today.

Copper wires from Baldwin's plant carried 10,000 volts of juice down the canyon to light the town of Pomona fifteen miles away. Within three years, lines strung from the Folsom Power House on the American River delivered 11,000 volts eighteen miles to the state capital, whose citizens celebrated with a "grand electrical carnival" and a capitol outlined in electric bulbs. Mixing its metaphors, the *Sacramento Bee* proudly proclaimed, "Then Glowed the Sunlight of an Aurora of Progress and Prosperity," as illuminated trolley cars glided through triumphal arches.

By 1901, a plant on the Yuba River was sending high-voltage energy over 142 miles of line to Oakland. Such pioneer installations were followed by circuitry that quickly enmeshed the state, converting and carrying the power of Sierra rivers down to the cities, where it acted like a growth hormone. Along the way, that energy ran gold dredges and mines, reclamation pumps, factories, and ever more ingenious forms of farm machinery.

Heavy machinery is not what we generally choose to remember, however. The desire to rediscover a lost Arcadia or Eden is particularly strong in California, where the dream came briefly close to reality, thanks largely to just such machines and to the remote control technology that moved energy from where it was generated to where it could be used.

Contrary to common belief, electricity, rather than the automobile, created Los Angeles early in the twentieth century. Following Dr. Baldwin's experiment at Pomona, Henry Edwards Huntington brought electricity to the city on umbilical lines reaching as far as the San Joaquin River 240 miles to the north. No other single person, not even the Chandlers of the *Los Angeles Times,* did more to create southern California than Huntington.

Through an elaborately interlocked chain of corporations backed by his Southern Pacific inheritance and the access to the bankers that it gave him, Huntington set out to raise the value of his enormous landholdings. Electricity from his power plants ran an expanding network of streetcars and interurbans whose routes he deliberately designed to spread the city like a thin coverlet across his real estate. In 1904 an astonished tourist wrote home to his wife, "I have not seen a city so honeycombed by trolley lines as this is. They seem to run on nearly every street and they extend all over the surrounding country for miles. Some of the country lines run the cars a mile a minute."[2] Streetlights, houses, and commercial strips

Electrical carnival, Sacramento, 1895 (courtesy
Sacramento Archives and Museum Collection Center)

Opposite: Folsom Power House, Folsom, 1995

FOLSOM PIONEER
HYDROELECTRIC POWER PLANT

Water necessary for hydroelectric power at the Folsom Powerhouse was diverted by a dam located just downstream of the present Folsom Dam. This 89 foot high dam stretched 470 feet between the river gorge walls.

DAM

The canal connecting the dam to the powerhouse ran about two miles. Convicts built most of it using large granite rocks. Portions of the canal are still visible upstream on this side of the river.

CANAL

The forebay, located above the Powerhouse, allowed water from the canal to slow down so that sand and silt could settle to the bottom. This helped keep the "grit" from passing into and damaging the powerhouse machinery.

FOREBAY

Large pipes, called "penstocks", carried the water from the forebay 55 feet to the turbines (or waterwheels) below. There are four penstocks, each with a diameter of 8 feet.

PENSTOCKS

As water struck the double turbines, they turned the generators that produced electricity. After water fell from the turbine blades it passed through draft tubes and out under the building to the tailrace and back into the American River.

WHEEL ROOM

The four General Electric generators delivered a potential of 800 volts, making it the most powerful hydroelectric plant in July of 1895. Standing 9 feet high and weighing in excess of 57,000 pounds, these generators were shipped around Cape Horn from the East Coast.

GENERATOR ROOM

A switchboard connected power from the generators to outgoing powerlines. This board was faced with two inches of Tennessee marble, which prevented electric currents from passing through it.

SWITCHBOARD

On July 13, 1895, the Powerhouse made history by being the first plant in the United States to successfully transmit high-voltage electricity (11,000 volts) over a long distance (22 miles to Sacramento) for commercial use.

POWER LINES

Griffith Park Observatory and the grid of city lights at dusk, Los Angeles, 1993

followed the trolley lines into the countryside. From the 5,700-foot summit of Mount Wilson, Angelenos looked down at night upon the expanding grid of illumination that Huntington was building. Nothing like it had ever been seen before. It heralded the limitless, horizontal megalopolis of the twentieth century.

Huntington made Los Angeles an electrified paradise and advertised it through the Southern Pacific's promotional organ, *Sunset* magazine. Filled with seductive articles and illustrations, *Sunset* promised that the world's most highly developed interurban trolley system would, for the first time, make possible the democratization in miniature of what had previously been available only to the rich—the country estate.

A 1913 article entitled "The Red Car of Empire," for example, followed a fictional shoe merchant's family through a typical day made idyllic by a unique combination of balmy climate and high voltage. The merchant commuted speedily and cheaply between downtown and his home in an orange grove in the midst of meadows. Mother did her shopping the same way, her time freed by home appliances. On weekends and in the evenings, the family enjoyed trolley excursions on a thousand-mile network of tracks running from mountain to beach resorts through groves of sweetly scented orange trees. Work in Los Angeles, for those who did it, was a joy, according to *Sunset.* "Southern California is to become—rather, it is becoming—the playground of the world. The leisure idea is as unmistakable as the climate."[3]

Many had reason to believe that the city and nature would at last be reconciled in a happy marriage of both. "Delightful little home-made cottages of redwood are to be found all through California," wrote Los Angeles architect Irving Gill in 1916. He called them "homes of the future," and added that "they cost their owners but a few hundred dollars. . . . Everybody has one and lives therein hap-

pier than any king, enjoying a simple, free, healthy life, breathing eucalyptus and pine-scented air, resting full-length in a flower starred grass, bathing in the fern-bordered streams." Allowing for the usual exaggeration, the electrified California bungalow and trolley did provide a level of ease for the common man virtually unknown before. Gill, however, did not know that his "homes of the future" were doomed by the very economic forces that had built them.[4]

Colored postcards and plates in *Sunset* deliberately aimed images of bungalows, pergolas, and flowering fruit trees at residents of Iowa and New England in the dead of winter. So did citrus crate labels, which added castles in Spain, peacocks, and saucy señoritas as inducements to move on out to the Pacific coast. Hollywood movies spread the gospel of easy living for the benefit of studio moguls and stars heavily invested in land speculation. Small wonder that by 1911, Los Angeles builders were laying out four and a half miles of palm-lined street per month with houses that frugal working men and widows could afford on easy terms. Developers often laid electric lines underground with the gas mains, allowing residents to forget the essential role that those systems played in providing for their comfort and safety. Tracts replaced orange groves with increasing speed as newcomers poured in to boost the value of land owned by Huntington and his associates.

Those who bought flower-bowered bungalows in the midst of orchards quickly acquired neighbors as the energy-engorged city swept outward at breakneck speed. Builders backfilled meadows, orchards, and farms, all of which were swallowed up by the city's frenzied growth. Irving Gill's "fern-bordered streams" soon became trash-filled sewers and flood threats. The paradise promised to everyman consumed itself. Only the wealthiest, such as Huntington on his 200-acre estate in San Marino, could afford to keep the city at bay.

T. D. Keith Residence, South Pasadena (courtesy Huntington Library, San Marino, California)

Fruit crate label (courtesy Oakland Museum of California)

Looking down on spray, Shasta Dam, 1995

Yet still, to a degree, it appeared to work, for the long-distance transmission of electricity distanced the consequences of its production. Gone was the local coal yard, coal cellar, and coal-burning locomotive, and with them the smoke and stench that those in the nineteenth century took as a good and sure sign of prosperity. Boosters dubbed hydroelectric energy "white coal" and promised a new age of cleanliness and convenience that machines seemed to deliver.

Up in the canyons of the Sierra and the San Bernardinos, "hydro" proved not quite so benign. Ever-larger dams drowned valleys and canyons. In 1924 a bizarre incident illustrated what was happening to the state's streams as concrete choked them off. So many Yuba River salmon piled themselves against the base of the new Bullards Bar Dam that Pacific Gas and Electric workmen had to torch them with gasoline to alleviate the stench. Deprived of their breeding grounds, salmon soon ceased to be a nuisance. San Francisco's attempt to dam Hetch Hetchy Valley in Yosemite National Park for power and water ignited a nationwide furor, but in virtually every other instance, the utilitarian position won with little dissent.

Still, the state's hydroelectric reservoirs are only as good as the precipitation that reaches the state from the sea. Drought cripples them. But in the same year that Dr. Baldwin initiated hydroelectric transmission to Pomona, a nomadic prospector named Edward Doheny found a source of energy that appeared to free the state from the vagaries of Pacific storms and from the limitations of fuel wood. He found it directly beneath Los Angeles.

Tar seeps had long been known to occur throughout California, while oil wells produced a limited amount of heavy crude used for lighting and lubrication. Doheny sank a shaft, then drilled into some seeps that oozed up on Second Street just east of downtown. At a depth of six hundred feet he hit oil, setting off a frantic boom

Oil wells and mansion, Signal Hill (courtesy Huntington Library, San Marino, California)

Oil derricks, McKittrick, 1993

that soon covered that and other Los Angeles neighborhoods with a dense and stinking forest of derricks, tanks, and refineries. Two years later, Los Angeles was producing 729,000 barrels of oil annually, and production was rising.

The adjective "sleepy" no longer applied to the suddenly energy-rich city. Floating on a sea of fossil fuel, the Los Angeles economy leapt forward and its borders outward. No longer would its industries be handicapped by a lack of good coal or the droughts that stanched hydroelectricity, for prospectors discovered even larger pools of energy trapped by tectonic forces in the folds of the Coast Range and across the southern end of the San Joaquin Valley. Oil, too, lay off the beaches of Ventura and Santa Barbara Counties. By the turn of the century, the town of Bakersfield was booming on the mighty Kern River fields.

Side by side with the electrical grid grew a system of pipes to carry liquid energy and gas from the fields to the refineries. In 1902, John D. Rockefeller's Standard Oil Company completed a 280-mile long pipeline from the Bakersfield wells to a deep-water port on San Francisco Bay. With an abundance of cheap energy suddenly available at the end of the pipe, Richmond sprang to life in a marsh, promising further fortunes in real estate speculation. Standard Oil built one of the world's largest refineries there, and another at El Segundo in west Los Angeles.

By 1909, California was supplying 80 percent of the nation's fuel oil, and yet there was still too much, and more coming on line every year. The following two decades saw a series of spectacular gushers that at times threatened to overwhelm and capsize the industry. A spokesman lamented that the industry was cursed by its own good fortune: "We are being choked and strangled, and gagged by the very thing most wanted—oil!"[5] By 1923, California produced up to a quarter of all the world's petroleum.

The stuff could, of course, simply be fed into the existing power grid to run public transit at central generating stations like Huntington's Redondo Beach plant, but those who owned it knew they would have to create a virtually insatiable hunger for petroleum if it were to retain its reputation as "black gold" and oil stocks their value on the market. A newly invented form of private transportation furnished a far better way than trolleys to use it up.

The fledgling public relations industry got to work selling the automobile to folks like the fictional Los Angeles shoe merchant, who was otherwise happy with the streetcar. Newspapers, movies, and *Sunset* ballyhooed the private car both for its convenience and as the ideal means of escape from growing city cares. Top down and filled with carefree revelers, automobiles posed against backdrops of Yosemite Valley, Lake Tahoe, Navajo reservations, and, of course, the ubiquitous orange groves and snow-capped mountain ranges of southern California. The car became as synonymous with freedom and civil liberties as the private firearm.

Its growing popularity helped to sell still more cars, as Californians discovered traffic jams, car crashes, billboards, exhaust, and a steadily rising level of noise—new forms of stress from which the car promised escape. To get back to the peace of nature, drivers would need near-infinite amounts of gasoline, lubricants, and asphalt to carry them there.

The automobile thus increased the development potential of rural land, opening steep hillside sites previously inaccessible to streetcars. It became, in fact, the most perfect tool ever devised for increasing the value of real estate while simultaneously keeping the price of oil up. Energy use rose gratifyingly; had they chosen to do so, the physicists at Pasadena's Cal Tech could have calculated a person's social status by the number of BTUs he consumed daily.

Ishi consumed relatively few in his simple room at the museum

IN GOLDEN GATE PARK, SAN FRANCISCO

LIFE'S BEST MIXTURE: SUN AND AIR AND GASOLINE

IN THESE CITIES, WHERE NO SLEET OR ICICLE-POINTED WIND HARRIES THE BUSY LIFE OF THE STREETS IN THE ENCHANTED WINTER SEASON, AND WHERE FLOWER VENDORS LINE THE CURBS, THE ROADS THROUGH MAGNIFICENT THOUSAND-ACRE PARKS FEEL THE SWIFT PRESSURE OF MOTOR CARS WHICH NEVER KNOW WHAT IT IS TO BE SHUT AWAY IN WINTER STORAGE

Sunset *magazine illustration: "Life's Best Mixture—*
Sun and Air and Gasoline," December 1912

overlooking Golden Gate Park. He was, in fact, losing energy to a disease traditionally associated with overcrowding. Tuberculosis killed him in 1916, but the year before he died, the last Yahi was able to visit a world's fair built on the shores of San Francisco Bay.

The Panama-Pacific International Exposition of 1915 advertised the dawning age of clean and plentiful power and the growing consumption that it encouraged. The fair's crowds were enormous; more than 19 million people visited the PPIE during its ten-month run. Visitors marveled at a myriad of appliances and products that would radically change their lives and those of their children. They saw models of oil wells and refineries and the dynamos that promised limitless force without pollution. They wandered at night through a fairytale city that glowed with soft, indirect lighting free of smoke.

From the Marina Green, they could see smoke by day and fires by night issuing from another kind of city across the bay. Over in Contra Costa County, an expanding sprawl of factories, chemical works, smelters, and explosives plants grew at the outlet of the Bakersfield pipeline. Richmond's workers and their families lived under a perpetual lid of petrochemical distillates and the constant danger of explosive accidents and toxic leaks, while executives built their estates upwind. Few of the fair's visitors crossed the water to view Richmond, but a congressional committee did take a few hours to inspect a boulevard lined with colossal brick stills, grimy pipes, belching chimneys, and high-tension lines. They found it emblematic of national progress and prosperity, then quickly returned to the fair.

An even larger industrial zone grew around the oil fields of west Los Angeles after the discovery of the Signal Hill bonanza in 1921. With a peak daily production of 250,000 barrels from that one field alone, the model towns of Torrance and Venice vanished in yet an-

House being moved from new oil fields in Inglewood (courtesy Huntington Library, San Marino, California)

other wilderness of derricks and tanks. West Los Angeles grew rank with the stench of oil. An observer called the area at the mouth of the Los Angeles River "a stygian landscape," which had an unfortunate tendency to erupt in flame, engulfing entire neighborhoods. Oil dimmed the air over the city, hiding the mountains and fueling more growth at the edges. The workers who lived there complained that oil permeated everything, sickened their children, killed their fruit trees, drenched vegetable gardens, and devastated the creeks and beaches.[6]

Two world wars did much to hasten the exhaustion of the state's underground energy. At their most basic, wars are simply spasms of energy spent in hopes of acquiring more. As the greatest such convulsion to date, World War II was fittingly climaxed by the release of a new form of energy whose potential seemed at last to justify

Oil well fire, Santa Fe Springs (courtesy Huntington Library, San Marino, California)

View from Signal Hill of oil derrick and Long Beach, 1995

the overworked adjective "limitless." A few saw in the fireballs that rose over Hiroshima and Nagasaki the hope of a new age in which humanity would be able to rearrange the earth to its own benefit. California, whose state university had done so much to produce the bomb, might serve as a laboratory for the peaceful use of atomic fission.

Atomic energy appeared in the nick of time, for on May 11, 1949, Governor Earl Warren announced that California was running out of fuel. The state must, he said, develop all sources available to accommodate anticipated growth, for it was no longer self-sufficient. Its oil production peaked on January 1 of that year, and from then on it would need to import energy. By doing so, its economics and politics became necessarily and inextricably entangled with those of the Middle East, Venezuela, Indonesia, and Mexico.

Small wonder that power experts forecast as many as ninety nuclear reactors strung along the coast at ten-mile intervals, for energy demand seemed to grow exponentially with the postwar prosperity that spurred it on. Public utilities launched advertising campaigns to persuade their customers to buy an exciting array of high-voltage appliances, while auto makers equated car size with luxury, status, and futuristic modernity. The new glass-walled buildings, which behaved precisely like the greenhouses that inspired them, created a voracious demand for the energy necessary to keep them habitable. Mechanized agribusiness consumed still more.

Aerial view of Oildale, 1991

To a degree that few were aware of at the time, the growing demand for energy—which was virtually synonymous with the word "progress"—was planned. Auto, oil, tire, and construction companies rhapsodized over the freedom of the new freeways that led out to the retreating countryside, as they themselves lobbied relentlessly to have those freeways built. To ensure that consumers would make the progressive choice, they conspired to convince the nation's transit riders that their electrically powered systems were obsolete and that they should junk them.

Through front companies and compliant politicians, they bought up transit systems and hastened their decay. Against vehement protests, they dismantled the East Bay's Key Route and Marin County's Northwestern Pacific. I watched the workmen rip up the rails of the interurban that ran through Los Altos and replace it with the Foothill Expressway. Consultants recommended scrapping what little remained of San Francisco's cable cars. Huntington's Los Angeles transit empire withered and vanished. Some of the systems were replaced with diesel buses, which their makers billed as the very last word in modernity and comfort. When it was over, commuters had little choice but to consume fossil fuel. The freedom of the road had become its tyranny.

California's petrochemical landscapes remain among its most impressive, yet they are as little visited as Richmond during the 1915 world's fair because they so directly refute the image of paradise that plentiful energy promises elsewhere. Coming upon the Kern River fields in a small plane, we saw an unearthly country stretching off to a hazy horizon north of Bakersfield. Only machines moved through the rural counterpart to the state's urban refineries. Steam rose from injection wells and contributed to the infernal quality of the place, while pools of tar reflected the sun like viscous obsidian in a gashed wilderness of conduits, pumps, and rusted condensers.

Oil soaks the hard-living towns of Oildale, Taft, and McKittrick, where workers drift in from the Texas and Oklahoma fields to suck out what remains in the underground pools. It's a dying way of life, for the oil promoters in the first half of the century succeeded all too well in maintaining the price of oil by using up California's vast fuel reserves. The men who tore up the streetcars did much to deliver the coup de grâce.

Unfortunately for those who predicted a new era of limitless power, nuclear energy turned out to be a mirage. Popular resistance to "atomic parks" grew with accidents and revelations of the dangers associated with reactors. Extended legal battles and regulations have succeeded in internalizing the long-term costs of nuclear energy to a greater degree than for any other industry, making it expensive and closing several California plants. In addition to the chances for a catastrophic failure, there remains the unanswered problem of what to do with the radioactive materials that reactors both demand and generate in prodigious quantities. The search for a permanent sacrifice zone to sequester what has already been produced remains one of the nation's—and the world's—longest-running dilemmas.

Meanwhile, few Californians realize the threat to the state's existence posed by the scarcity of energy, and hence by its rising cost. By the mid-1990s, gas-intensive sport-utility vehicles had become hot fashion statements symbolic of freedom, while tourists packed Las Vegas to experience dazzling diversions of electricity. The energy crisis of 1973 and the Gulf War of 1991 by then seemed ancient history.

Not only do Niagaras of cheap petroleum move Californians daily about the country, but those same rivers are converted into their food and exports. Energy is inextricably linked with another necessity of life, for enormous quantities are required simply to

Ward Valley sign, Ward Valley, 1996

force water to go wherever it will raise crops, livestock, and land values. California's greatest electrical demand today is for the pumps that suck water from the Delta, then shove it uphill to a station near Bakersfield where even bigger pumps lift it more than three-thousand feet over the Tehachapi Mountains. Probably no such tenuous experiment in energy-induced growth has ever been tried, yet without the cheap power that drives that river against the force of gravity, agribusiness and the cities of southern California would soon cease to exist.

Much of the power needed to move water through the State Water Project comes from the turbines at Oroville Dam, whose lake, like other Sierra reservoirs, is filling with the debris of mining, logging, road-building, and other human activities. The electricity begins its journey south through wires carried by tall steel pylons. They swing in catenary arcs over the site of the corral where barking dogs in 1911 alerted a rancher to a man dying for want of energy. For the moment, they feed the crowds that so astonished that man. They also power the illusion that the entire state can be made a city.

Power lines across flooded field, Sacramento Valley, 1986

Aerial view of wind farm, Altamont Pass, 1986

Solar panels, Carrizo Plain, 1989

Faded California movie marquee, San Diego, 1992

FIVE: ALABASTER CITIES

"Could you mistake Italy for California?" a woman I met on a train passing through Tuscany once asked me. Their climates, vegetation, and topography are similar enough. Classically educated writers used to say that such a Mediterranean environment fated Californians to repeat the glories of Greco-Roman civilization. Instead, Italy is now copying the mistakes pioneered by Californians.

I thought of that question often as Bob and I moved through the state observing its cities and the farmlands vanishing beneath them. No, I'd said to the woman on the train, for Italians loved their towns and the countryside around them and carefully cultivated both to a such a degree that Italy, in the age of jumbo jets, became one of the chief tourist destinations for refugees from what Americans have made of their own land. Small cities such as Siena, Spoleto, and Lucca are known worldwide as centers of urbane living and masterful town planning. The same can hardly be said for Modesto, El Centro, or San Jose.

That is because Californians, as novelist Frank Norris said, did not love their land or even regard it as such. Instead, they made it an interchangeable commodity that could be bought and sold on the market like cuts of meat, with the sirloin tip of real estate being the lots that underlie growing cities.

Whereas Italians attempted to create *civitas*, the Latin word for community and the root of civilization itself, Californians have repeatedly attempted to escape the problems that inevitably arise in unloved cities by discarding them like outgrown shells and building elsewhere, preferably on cheap peripheral farmland. In the process of that eternal escape, they have produced towns that resemble nothing so much as bread mold spreading in time-lapse across a landscape consumed by their demands.

We flew over the coalesced cities of southern California on a day blown clear by an approaching storm. From a mile up, the apparent limits of that world metropolis are defined by the coastal mountains, the Pacific shoreline, and the curve of the earth. It is easy to spot the highest-value real estate by the height of buildings rising from the gridded plain; glass towers proliferate at the important intersections, which not long ago were the corners of farms. Wilshire Boulevard has become a double palisade of highrises running eighteen miles from the Santa Monica beaches to downtown. Those who

111

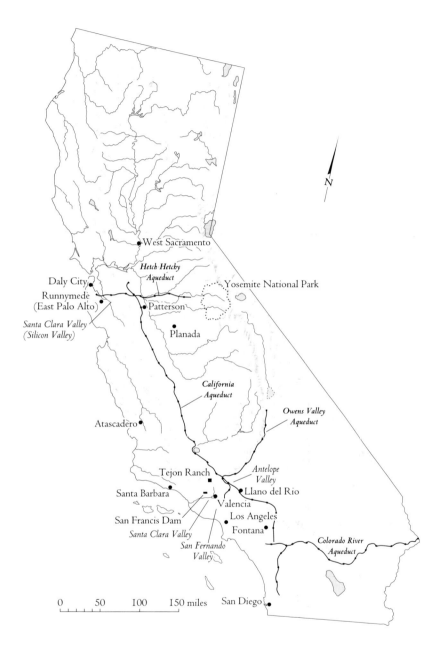

Ideal Cities

claim that Los Angeles has no center have not seen the new downtown, which gathers itself to the side of the old one, now abandoned to the poor and the dark. Its sleek spires rise sixty stories from the stump of a fashionable Victorian neighborhood known as Bunker Hill. From any point in the basin, one's eyes turn automatically to that center of power as to a glacier-clad volcano. All the rest seems infinite suburb to it.

At that height, you can hear the roar of the city in motion punctuated by the wail of sirens responding to emergencies. Fed by its pools of oil, California produced mobility rather than *civitas*. We flew over the blackened wreckage of South Central L.A., whose residents rioted in the spring of 1992 and threatened to burn down the rest of the city.

Deep beneath the neighborhoods of South Central lie what remains of the energy bonanzas that laid the foundations of both old and new downtowns. Money flowed out of the 'hoods with far less viscosity than the heavy crude pumped from the wells, leaving behind a landscape short on glamour and long on rage and despair. I remembered the smoke drifting north to Santa Barbara as Highway 101 jammed with refugees fleeing the burning city.

We flew over the petrochemical works at Torrance and El Segundo, the tank farms and oil wells, and the Hyperion—the world's largest sewage treatment plant—whose gigantic capacity is strained by the metabolic wastes produced by the city's ceaseless growth. We saw the gutted industrial plants mixed with decayed housing, the mile after mile of dying and toxic tissue near the geographic heart of Los Angeles that tries, futilely, to grow away from itself. In this it is no different from most other California cities.

Where the Santa Monica, San Bernardino, and San Gabriel Mountains once acted as levees to confine the megalopolis to lowlands stretching from Malibu to the Mexican border, it now spills through the passes and spreads out into the valleys and across the deserts to the east. Anticipating its arrival, developers gridded the sagebrush plains of Antelope Valley across the San Gabriels. Street signs reach out from Palmdale numbering into the high two-hundreds, waiting for the water, energy, freeways, and buyers that will give the desert value. Over the hill from the legendary sprawl of the San Fernando Valley, a new city called Valencia is filling the Santa Clara Valley using the popular selling point that it is not Los Angeles. Twenty miles beyond Valencia, the Chandler family has sold its quarter-million acre Tejon Ranch in the Tehachapi Mountains to developers.

Once, far to the east, we watched the lights of an unbroken stream of cars across a soda lakebed. They defined the freeway connecting Los Angeles with Las Vegas, whose high-voltage fantasy throws a false dawn over the eastern horizon at midnight. Promoters hope to build the nation's first magnetic-levitation (maglev) bullet train between Disneyland and Vegas, the twin poles of escape from American reality. Watching the traffic, we knew that if developers can find water and energy enough, the Mojave Desert will be city in time, its silence and starfields joining the absence of so many other things.

All evidence to the contrary, editorials in such major newspapers as the *San Francisco Chronicle* continue to speak of the "natural and healthy" growth of California cities which, they sagely advise, we must collectively plan for.[1] California's cities seldom grew "naturally," however, or with the avowed purpose of providing deserving citizens with housing and work. With the unwitting aid of taxpayers, a few determined individuals have irrigated, seeded, and grown them like cash crops in the desert; it is no accident that the Chandler family's *Los Angeles Times* long stood between City Hall and the De-

partment of Water and Power, mediating the influence of both to the advantage of the newspaper's owners.

From the fortress of his *Times* headquarters, General Harrison Gray Otis and his son-in-law Harry Chandler shaped what the city would become. They had every reason to relentlessly hawk southern California as the Garden of Eden, for they owned huge tracts of investment property extending from Tejon Pass well into Mexico. They took particular interest in a 17,000-acre spread in the dusty San Fernando Valley north of downtown, whose ownership they shared with other developers, such as streetcar titan Henry Huntington and Edward Harriman, the president of the Southern Pacific Railroad.

The San Fernando land syndicate needed engineers as well as promotion if it was to turn raw land into real estate. The syndicate was fortunate, for Los Angeles had if not the best engineer, certainly one of the best known for getting things done. Bill Mulholland first saw the Los Angeles River when, in 1877, he came poor from Ireland. It then filled him with joy: "The Los Angeles River," he later recalled, "was the greatest attraction. It was a beautiful, limpid little stream with willows on its banks. . . . It was so attractive to me that it at once became something about which my whole scheme of life was woven. I loved it so much."[2]

Mulholland's love, however, was incompatible with the river's supply. It could never slake the ambitions of the Chandlers and their partners, who thought in terms bigger than a town of 200,000, which is about all that its modest and fickle flow could support. Following a rousing scare campaign, voters passed a bond issue to build an aqueduct, and in 1913 Mulholland brought in another river, one from the Owens Valley, 233 miles away. The taxpayer-funded growth that it spawned soon made even the Owens River insufficient, and

Odd Fellows' arch, "Faith, Hope, and Charity," Fresno (photo Maxwell & Mudge, courtesy California Historical Society, FN-30649)

Corporate arch, Pleasanton, 1992

Aerial view of the urban grid, Los Angeles, 1993

Water — the destiny of a Mighty Empire hangs in the balance Now!

Yesterday

Artesian Wells

Abundant water

Dry

Today

120 to 350 ft. to Water

Rapidly dropping water level

Dry

EMPIRE BUILDERS again face the age-old problem of water in Southern California . . . Behind lies the bright chronicle of achievement of the Padre, the Don, the Forty-niner and the Pioneer . . . Ahead the dream of untold greatness.

But today—

Rapidly dropping water levels—a problem we must solve if we are to maintain this great empire, to say nothing of future development. The only solution is the Colorado River Aqueduct.

Southern California stands at the cross-roads. Unmolested for countless centuries before the coming of the Padres, Nature filled the underground basins of the coastal plain with water. Now, we are exhausting this supply by using 200,000,000 gallons a day *more than is being replaced by man or Nature*. All available local water supplies are and will be developed to their fullest extent. We know these supplies are inadequate, and now the one, the *only* remaining source is the Colorado River . . .

WE MUST BUILD THE COLORADO RIVER AQUEDUCT . . . NOW!

A map of the giant Colorado River Aqueduct which is to span the state, bringing a new and adequate water supply to the thirteen member-cities of the Metropolitan Water District of Southern California. Stars indicate the cities now in the District.

Ad in support of the Colorado River Aqueduct, La Fiesta de Los Angeles program, 1931 (courtesy Huntington Library, San Marino, California)

Aberdeen ditch sending water to Los Angeles aqueduct, Owens Valley, 1992

so Mulholland laid the groundwork for importing the Colorado River across the Mojave Desert, and the Sacramento River over the Tehachapi Mountains. Those, too, have proved too paltry for the demands of southern California's developers. Mulholland's successors dream of getting the Columbia, the Yukon, and the rivers of Canada.

Imported water turned San Fernando soil into gold. The influx of settlers, far more than their newspaper, made the Chandlers among the wealthiest and most powerful Americans. They molded the region to their own ends, seldom, if ever, pondering the ul-

timate consequences of unlimited growth. Their wealth insulated them from life on the ground, while the L.A. police were there to quell any doubts in the minds of either the powerful or the lowly.[3]

In this the Chandlers were no different from other publishers who have used their dailies to promote a state of which they owned so much. The Hearst, Spreckels, deYoung, Knowland, and Lesher families all strove to attract more immigrants to raise the value of their properties. As the Chandlers worked closely with Huntington, so did other publishers maintain intimate relations with developers, bankers, and real estate men. In the north, borax magnate F. M.

Los Angeles aqueduct flowing above Ellen and Walker, Owens Valley, 1992

Smith, banker William Crocker, and many others attempted to re-peat the success of the San Fernando syndicate by turning San Fran-cisco and its suburbs into a copy of Los Angeles. If that meant rid-ding the Bay Area of the bay, it would simply have to go.

Though the costs of growth were seldom mentioned in the cease-less media hype, Mulholland's own radical alterations in the state's hydrology had side effects he should have anticipated. No longer needed for drinking water as the urban grid closed about it, the Los Angeles River became the city's trunk sewer. Moreover, its mean-dering course defied the linear abstraction that surveyors laid over it. The river's flood plain took up valuable space better converted from truck farms to industrial zones. In 1938 the Army Corps of Engineers straightened the channel and armored it in a trapezoidal shell of concrete.

As much as Henry Huntington's gardens in San Marino represent one face of civilization, the Los Angeles River shows another. A stark incision devoid of trees or any other sign of green, it slices through railroad marshaling yards past grimy warehouses and factories, tank farms, container storage yards, and piles of sulfur. High-tension lines follow it for much of its course through South Central to a

Owens Valley water leaving Owens Valley and arriving in Los Angeles (diptych), 1989

Sweeping Back the Flood

When John Muir and the Sierra Club opposed plans to dam Hetch Hetchy Valley in Yosemite National Park, San Francisco newspapers depicted the revered naturalist as an effete enemy of progress and of the city itself. San Francisco Call, *December 13, 1909 (courtesy Bancroft Library)*

Pipe containing most of San Francisco's water supply, near Mather, 1992

harbor at Long Beach so toxic it kills the barnacles on ship hulls anchored there. Shantytowns resembling those of the world's most impoverished nations grow along its banks, and in the summer, the destitute bathe in the swill running down its center. Movie crews use it for high-speed chase scenes. Whenever I see it, I cannot help but wonder what Mulholland would think about the willow-lined stream he loved so well, and did so much to kill.

It did not have to be that way. Given concerns for *civitas* as well as a longer perspective than what rapid turnover of real estate demands, California cities could have grown differently. In 1905 city planner Daniel Burnham recommended that San Francisco reserve its largest stream, Islais Creek, as a public park near its southern

Sunol Water Temple, Sunol, 1987

Pulgas Water Temple, Crystal Springs Lake, 1987

Islais Creek disappearing into city sewer, Glen Canyon Park, San Francisco, 1995

Converting Islais Creek into a sewer, San Francisco, 1925 (collection of Greg Gaar), and same view in 1986 showing Highway 280 over former creek bed

border. A greenbelt would, Burnham admitted, use valuable real estate, but the park would ultimately serve the needs of those who would eventually live nearby. The city took no action, and the valley quickly filled with a dense working-class neighborhood that polluted the creek. Instead of a park, the stream was buried as a nuisance, and the marsh at its mouth was filled for an industrial zone.

The city health board condemned cabbages irrigated with its water and bay shrimp taken near its mouth. Later, the State Division of Highways laid the Junipero Serra Freeway on top of it. Today it is a realm of the city too drab for tourists or movie companies to visit.

Burnham was by no means alone, for in the same year that Mulholland turned his water onto the San Fernando Valley, the city of

Berkeley asked German planner Werner Hegemann to develop a comprehensive plan for the cities of the East Bay. Hegemann's 1915 report went far beyond Burnham's cosmetic recommendations for San Francisco. He envisioned a humane and efficient whole entirely at odds with the haphazard tradition of western growth. He, too, proposed that the cities protect their watersheds and create park chains along all their creeks so that no one—rich or poor—need be far from greenbelts connecting the bay to the hills. Though few of his parks were realized, Hegemann's hopes were bolstered by simultaneous events in San Francisco and San Diego. California that year hosted two world's fairs to celebrate the opening of the Panama Canal. Both created ideal cities fit for pedestrians. They

Two years into a six-year drought, Pine Flat Reservoir (diptych), 1988

Aerial view of flooded town, Central Valley, 1986

Aerial view of canal, Central Valley, 1991

Tunnel, Feather River, 1987

Exchequer Dam, near Merced, 1985

Pardee Dam, 1995

Top: *Aerial view of O'Shaughnessy Dam, 1991*

Bottom: *Aerial view of Oroville Dam, 1986*

seemed the realization, at last, of all that promoters promised for California.

San Francisco's Panama-Pacific Exposition, which Ishi visited in his last year, was by far the larger. Its waterfront colonnades, palm-lined boulevards, sculptures, gardens, and fountains stood symbolically for what the city claimed to be while denying what so much of it had become. Unabashedly imperial, the plaster fair lasted just ten months before it was pulled down to make way for speculative housing.

San Diegans staged their Panama-California Exposition in a public park and kept the structures after the fair closed. The exposition was more intimate than San Francisco's and, in keeping with the town's mythology, more Spanish colonial than Roman imperial. It is there in Balboa Park that one can begin to understand the optimism of the time. Along The Prado stand the museums and meeting halls that led visionaries at the time to predict that California was destined to become a world center of the arts and education. Freed by machines and gifted with enlightened leisure, its citizens would show the way for less fortunate places. Both fairs provided examples of what enlightened planning and public investment could accomplish for the greater good; they inspired love in those who saw them, and in some, a determination to do better in the future.

The mere announcement of the fairs set off a virtual renaissance of town planning throughout the state. Planada, near Merced, was "laid down on lines approved by modern civic improvement societies, its streets radiating from a common center, its buildings uniform in beauty and following a general architectural scheme." Its planners provided for ample parks, Spanish bungalows, and stately boulevards named after the members of a Los Angeles syndicate that financed the town.[4] Much the same was planned for West Sacramento, and for the model workers' community of Torrance near

*Street with symbols of early development
in impoverished town, Planada, 1993*

Los Angeles's harbor. In the coastal marshes next to Torrance, millionaire Abbott Kinney dug canals for a Venice that, he promised, would improve on its Old World namesake. *Sunset* claimed that the lushly landscaped "royal roads" that the San Fernando land syndicate laid across its lands would compel the new towns and suburban farms to live up to their magnificence. Approached by a four-mile palm-lined boulevard from docks on the San Joaquin River, the farming town of Patterson took its cue from the radial streets of Paris and Washington, D.C. Halfway down the El Camino Real,

promoter Edward Gardner Lewis bought the 23,000-acre Atascadero Rancho and advertised his Atascadero Colony as a permanent world's fair, with enough space allotted each house to make it self-sufficient in food production. Socialists founded a model community in the Antelope Valley called Llano del Rio. More modestly, Runnymede promised "an acre of land and independence" on south San Francisco Bay.

For all their beauty, both expositions functioned as trade shows whose overriding concern was to entice more immigrants to Cali-

Bird's-eye view of West Sacramento as ideal city, 1913
(courtesy West Sacramento Land Co.)

Aerial view of radial streets, Patterson, 1996

fornia and more investment in what boosters repeatedly called the state's "boundless" resources. California's new Highway Commission rushed the paving of the highway linking San Francisco with San Diego and named it for the old mission road. El Camino Real, they said, would show off the state to motorists: "The Commissioners take the position that the great expositions are the entrance arches to California," said Commissioner N. D. Darlington; "California itself is the biggest exposition of all." Another authority crowed, "The Expositions will bring untold thousands to California; the things the state highway shows them and promises them will induce many of these visitors to send back home for their household goods."[5]

Many did, but of all the idealistic ventures from that period, almost nothing remains except a few streets too broad for the motels, truck stops, and mini-malls now lining them. Most plans collapsed in swindle and the vicissitudes of the market. A domed classical building of russet brick facing a colossal mall is about all that was left of the Atascadero Colony after Lewis was convicted of mail fraud. Promoters of West Sacramento went bankrupt in 1914, and the city became an industrial adjunct of the capital before Interstate 80 bypassed and killed large parts of it. Downtown Planada consists of a Broadway flanked by a few shuttered shops off the road to Yosemite, while Venice is more carney sideshow than Italian Renaissance. Of Llano del Rio, only a few ruined walls of cobble aggregate remain in the sagebrush. Aided by an influx of commuters from the Bay Area, Patterson has become a relatively prosperous town despite the death of the river that made its port, but Runnymede, reborn as East Palo Alto, has become famous for its drugs and violence. Only Santa Barbara, rebuilding itself after a 1925 earthquake, came close to realizing the promise of *civitas* by passing strict design guidelines and making generous provision for parks and museums.

How to explain the failure of so many projects in a state that has traditionally thrived on its success? Critics have long blamed the automobile for the plight of California's cities and towns, but that is too easy an out, we realized as we left the freeways that bypass and overfly the worst. Though cars are a major factor in the decline of central cities and of pedestrian scale, they cannot explain a poverty so widespread and profound, and so at odds with the popular image of wealth along the golden coast. Such conditions existed long before the first Ford rolled off the assembly line. As early as 1877 a Mexican visitor expressed his astonishment at what he found concealed by San Francisco's opulent facade: "Behind the palaces run filthy alleys, or rather nasty dungheaps without sidewalks or illumination, whose loiterers smell of the gallows." [6]

For every showplace Hillsborough, Belvedere, Malibu, and Pacific Palisades there exist dozens of nondestinations such as Taft, Crescent City, Mendota, and Compton. Together, they placed three-quarters of California's counties below the national income average by the mid-1990s, and one-sixth of its citizens—including 2 million children—in a chronic state of hunger. Their shuttered and shattered Main Streets belie the fortunes they produced to make refuges elsewhere.

Unlike the towns of Italy, California's were built almost exclusively for extraction; whether they produced oil, cotton, timber, or weapons, they remain much the same as the mining towns that planner Frederick Law Olmsted observed during the Civil War, peopled with the same cheap and ready source of labor of all races and nationalities. "The sojourning habit of the people," Olmsted said then, "is shown in their want of interest in the fixed qualities of the place." [7] He felt that *civitas* was impossible in California's landscape of transience and poverty.

Chief among the "fixed qualities of the place" ignored by Californians was its geology. Bill Mulholland did so with results that made him declare late in life that he envied the dead. As water czar of the Los Angeles Department of Water and Power, Mulholland was kept so busy designing and building the vast network of aqueducts, reservoirs, and power plants that propelled southern California's growth that he had little time to reflect on its ultimate end. Some say he became overconfident, others that his self-taught engineering skills were not up to the magnitude of the projects he undertook. His champions said that Owens Valley farmers sabotaged his work. Near midnight on March 12, 1928, Mulholland's heroic prestige collapsed when his St. Francis Dam blew out at full capacity. The pooled waters of the Owens River exploded down southern California's Santa Clara Valley, scouring the topsoil and hurling the mangled wreckage of towns, orchards, and hundreds of bodies into the Pacific at dawn.

William Mulholland Memorial Fountain,
Los Angeles, 1995

Opposite: *Kids and grafitti, Pittsburg, 1987*

No plaque marks the site of the greatest of California's many dam failures, but the twenty-foot shards of rebar-embedded concrete we found resting in a meadow a mile below the dam's stump testify to the force of the flood.

Mulholland's tragedy was but a foretaste of an ever-greater chain of catastrophes as developers built out the grid in willful ignorance, or defiance, of the land's fixed qualities. As California has become synonymous with fires, earthquakes, mudslides, and floods, insurance companies have been forced to redefine what constitutes a natural disaster for the sake of their own solvency. Developer Henry Doelger, for example, laid Daly City across the San Andreas fault just south of San Francisco. When a quake ruptured the ground during construction, his bulldozers smoothed the break and he kept on building. He spent his last years in the Mediterranean on a succession of yachts he called *The Westlake;* it was named for a neighborhood on the bluffs, where today houses with spectacular views continue to toboggan into the Pacific.

By the 1990s, as drug addiction, crime, and fear spread from the big cities to small towns throughout the state, Californians searched for answers to their declining quality of life and the near-bankruptcy of their state. Memory is short, however, and perception selective in the land of tomorrow, and so they found answers in welfare moochers and lenient sentencing laws rather than in the poverty of towns they do not visit, or the consuming desires aroused by ubiquitous commercials, or the democratization of firearms. Nor do they connect present problems with three key ballot initiatives passed by voters who had little understanding of their long-term consequences.

Reflecting on his two-term administration in the go-go years of the 1960s, Governor Edmund G. ("Pat") Brown affably told an oral historian that citizens would never have voted for his State Water

Remnant of St. Francis Dam one mile downstream from dam site, seventy years after its collapse, near Los Angeles, 1993

Homes built on cliff, San Andreas Fault zone, Daly City, 1997

Project had they known its true cost. That he lied to get the SWP under way was by no means unusual, for such "misinformation" is commonly used by those who hope to be remembered or remunerated by gigantic public works, and Brown's water project was among the biggest. "I wanted this to be a monument to me," Brown admitted with a candor absent during his campaign for the project.[8] The public relations blitz at the time bore a striking resemblance to that used earlier by Otis and Chandler to persuade taxpayers to bring the Owens River to their land.

Under the illusion that the SWP would cost a mere $1.75 billion, California voters narrowly passed a bond measure to begin it on November 8, 1960.[9] In doing so, they unwittingly committed themselves in perpetuity to a project of staggering, unknown, and hidden expense. More predictably, they committed California to water- and energy-induced growth that would dwarf Mulholland's accomplishments. As before, the profits of that growth would largely go somewhere other than into the public treasury that funded it.

Since its completion, the 444-mile long California Aqueduct (officially named after his father by Governor Jerry Brown) has enabled some of the state's largest landholders, such as the multinational Kern County Land Company, to convert farm and ranch land into new cities. On the strength of the aqueduct, big-time developers laid out their streets in the Antelope Valley, and the Newhall family subdivided its hereditary holdings in the Santa Clara Valley to create Valencia. Crossing the Tejon Ranch, the aqueduct will also permit the ranch's owners to develop their strategic principality in the Tehachapis into what promoters call master-planned communities. The land barons have shown exemplary patience, for as early as 1920, a state engineering report stated that both the Kern County Land and the Tejon Ranch Companies needed an assured source of water for maximum development. Forty years later, the voters gave it to them.

Since few were willing or able to articulate the true costs of growth in terms of money or quality of life, it is hardly surprising that eighteen years after the authorization of the State Water Project the voters would opt to do something about their high property taxes by capping them at the polls. In 1978 they passed Proposition 13, thus firing the opening gun of the national tax revolt. Like the water project, it would have effects unknown for years to come.

Proposition 13's costs were long hidden by a multi-billion-dollar state surplus that did much to fuel voter ire. It took years to exhaust that surplus, and by the time it was gone, few connected the symptoms of an ailing state with the two earlier ballot measures. As it plunged toward insolvency, California had to drastically cut maintenance on its own infrastructure at the same time that its cities continued to feed and grow on SWP water. Those systems included not only the vital hardware of aqueducts and roads, but the software of culture and security that had once been California's pride—the very promise of civility embodied by the San Diego fair.

The slogan "do more with less" turned out to have practical limits. From 1978 to the 1990s, California school funding and achievement dropped in tandem from the nation's top five to near bottom. Half the school libraries closed at the same time that entire counties shut down or drastically curtailed public libraries and health facilities and reduced police and fire protection. By 1996 the state that boasts Silicon Valley had a ratio of students to computers that was second to last. Tuition and fees for the state's colleges and universities skyrocketed at the same time that their services plummeted. Strapped for cash, Los Angeles County began charging seventy-five-dollar fees for group picnics in its neglected parks. Orange County in 1994 staged the nation's greatest public bankruptcy and chose to default on more than $1.6 billion rather than raise its taxes. Indigence flourished, greatly augmented by the state's decision to close its mental institutions. A burgeoning street population of beggars and schizophrenics helped drive customers from downtown merchants. Almost every conceivable realm of public life contracted sharply, casting a grim tarnish across the Golden State. In growing numbers, those who could afford to escape did so. Others took drugs, or hired sentries and forted up.

By 1995, Las Vegas boasted that it was America's fastest-growing city, adding four thousand new residents per month to a watery wonderland in a blazing desert. Many were immigrants seeking abundant jobs, but many more were California emigrants fleeing the unadvertised costs of growth. In 1991, *Time* magazine devoted an entire issue to "California: The Endangered Dream," and in 1993 it ran a cover story that rhetorically asked, "Is the City of Angels Going to Hell?" [10] That, many Angelenos agreed, was precisely where Harry Chandler's paradise seemed to be headed.

Asked why they had left, ex-Californians recited the standard litany of symptoms: filthy air, teeth-grinding stress, lousy schools, beggars, earthquakes, fire, gridlock, and the high cost of housing. After the 1992 L.A. riots, worries about crime and violence topped the list. Real estate values dropped sharply. Almost three-fourths of those polled by the *Los Angeles Times* in 1992 called the city a bad place to raise children. A pregnant forest ranger we encountered erasing graffiti scrawled on the rocks in the San Bernardino Mountains concurred. She was willing, she said, to take a drastic cut in pay to get her kids out of southern California.

The 1993 kidnapping, rape, and strangulation of a pretty young girl in Petaluma not only symbolized much that has gone wrong with the California dream but galvanized popular determination to do something about it. Governor Pete Wilson wove Polly Klaas's murder into his 1994 State of the State address, which the *San Jose Mercury News* curtly summarized with the headline "Cut Taxes, Build Prisons." [11] Much to the puzzlement of his aides, the grim-faced governor promised tax relief and costly vengeance at the same time. He did not name a price for the latter.

Where fear was involved, however, cost was apparently no object. At Wilson's urging, the California legislature passed a law seconded by voters as an initiative requiring life sentences for criminals convicted of three offenses. The effects of Proposition 183 were seen sooner than those of previous measures. The bill for dozens of energy-intensive high-tech prisons appearing like brilliantly lit space stations on the backroads of the state quickly equaled and surpassed that for higher education, with which prisons had to compete for funding.

Unfortunately, the walls required by the "three strikes" initiative to imprison some made few on the outside feel any safer, for urban problems continue to grow with the cities themselves, and to follow emigrants trying to bail out. To an ever-greater degree, fear shapes the new towns of the affluent and pushes them farther from the discarded cores. At the same time, fear corrodes community as effectively as the automobile. A surreally empty medievalism pervades the walled suburban ghettos with their stucco chateaus and castles. They spring up in the remotest valleys of the state, where they will serve as spores for future cities. "Gated security" and armed sentries have joined hot tubs and golfing greens as a major selling point of today's master-planned communities.

In contrast, the walled cities of Italy teemed with the life of community. For all their greed, the magnates of those towns professed

FOR A BRIEF TIME"
"AN ANGEL RESTED HERE."
POLLY HANNAH KLAAS

Polly Klaas memorial, near Cloverdale, 1995

New prison and old courthouse, Madera, 1986

"No Trespassing" sign and new development, near Blackhawk, 1992

and practiced values more complex than those of real estate speculation. On the front of the Uffizi Gallery in Florence is a row of statues of many of the greatest figures in Western civilization. They portray the remarkable community of artists, scientists, philosophers, and architects that, for reasons no one has satisfactorily explained, flourished for over two centuries in a city whose population seldom exceeded 100,000. Perhaps it flourished because Italians imagined that cities could be works of art, and could make art of the lives of those who inhabit them. That, at least, was the hope of *civitas.*

It is, I have been told, unfair to compare Florence with our own cities, which increasingly take the form of identical shopping strips. Fontana, for example, is so far from an Italian city that the two may not belong to the same genus. We went there toward the end of our project to see Mike Davis's hometown. Davis had the dubious good fortune to publish what he called an "archaeology of the future" about Los Angeles shortly before the 1992 riots. His *City of Quartz* concluded with a chapter on the economic forces that make and break working-class towns like Fontana; he called it the "Junkyard of Dreams."

As Bob drove for miles past an endless procession of K-Marts, Burger Kings, Home Depots, car lots, and the gas stations that make it all possible, I could not stay awake, for I'd seen it so many times before. Amid such seeming abundance, the faces of those navigating the parking lots in the infernal atmosphere of the San Gabriel Valley bore the same signs of anxiety and loneliness we'd seen from Eureka to San Diego. Both the faces and the landscape reminded me of what had happened to my own hometown, and I, too, wanted to escape.

I watched a place once called the Santa Clara Valley change as dramatically as Davis's Fontana. Norman Mailer's response to an inquisitive reporter from the *San Jose Mercury News* did not, therefore, come as a surprise. Asked what he thought of Silicon Valley, the well-traveled writer replied that it depressed him immeasurably: "I think it's one of the ugliest places I've ever visited. It's abominable." There was irony, he said, in the singular lack of great buildings and public gestures. If we are, as Silicon Valley's boosters insist, experiencing a renaissance comparable to that begun in Florence, you'd never know it from the valley's leading city: "In a place where you have some of the most highly focused, concentrating minds in the country, you have the most mindless physical environment," said Mailer. "These sorts of buildings are part of the spiritual pollution we suffer, it's a species of pollution almost as bad as our poisoning of nature." [12]

The "spiritual pollution" of California's cities reflects the murder of nature required to build them. Both arise from the dream of limitless power that drives urban growth, and from the binding illu-

sion of freedom that those who wield energy promise to the dreamers in the parking lots. Both varieties of pollution contribute, too, to the decline in the health of the state.

Builder's cabin on Loma Prieta RR (photo Gil Filllian & Co., courtesy
California Historical Society, FN-29106)

Real estate sales office, East Bay, 1936 (photo by Dorothea Lange for the Farm Security Administration, courtesy Library of Congress)

Old shoreline marker, San Francisco, 1996

Removing the freeway, San Francisco, 1995

Houses on beach and storm detritus, Aptos, 1995

New homes being built on Mount San Bruno, South San Francisco, 1995

Overview of million-dollar homes, Blackhawk, 1992

Private property, Lake Tahoe, 1988

"This Community Is Protected by Smith-Wesson," sign near Chico, 1995

Security camera, downtown Los Angeles, 1992

Fountain, Caesar's Palace, Las Vegas—America's fastest-growing city, 1992

"Immortal Youth," San Francisco Call,
September 2, 1900 (courtesy California History Room,
California State Library, Sacramento)

"But thou shalt flourish in immortal youth," pledged the poppy-bordered caption to a full-page newspaper illustration of 1900. California was fifty years old that day, but the artist chose to depict the state not as the stern figure of Minerva seated on the state seal, but as a beautiful young giant in a loose gown blown by the sea wind. She stood on the hills above San Francisco Bay, her faced turned to the sun while a farmer plowed at her feet, the literal embodiment of health with which the state has long been identified.

Boosters had used just such images to attract more settlers and tourists to the Golden State. One could live forever in the promised land, they claimed, or at least be rejuvenated by moving there. The denial of mortality and of the ills to which flesh is heir forms a continuum of malarkey from the heroic Gold Rush miners to the blond and buffed surfers of today's Malibu. When New York reporter Bayard Taylor visited the state in the 1850s, he promised his readers they would find there the "dream of a more beautiful race in possession of this paradise—a race in which the lost symmetry and grace of the Greek was partially restored." He vowed to return

himself when old "to restore the sensations of youth in that wonderful air."[1]

Death itself could be banished in a land so richly endowed. In 1880, for example, the *San Francisco Post* declared war on the city's cemeteries: "[The dead] have seized and hold in mortmain the best building land in the city. . . . The development of the city is stopped short by these tyrants, who have placed themselves as an impassable barrier right in the natural path of the city's growth." Victorian piety yielded easily to the chance for enhanced land values; for the *Post*, the dead were no longer the dearly departed but rotting "tyrants" recruiting from the "lovely child flowers" who lived nearby.[2]

San Francisco kicked out its dead so the city could spread, but Los Angeles made them a tourist attraction. Shortly after the 1915 world's fairs, mining engineer Hubert Eaton transformed an old Glendale graveyard into a theme park with stress on Life Eternal and Celebrity Everlasting. Crowded with reproductions of famous monuments and works of art, Forest Lawn was less a cemetery than a preview of heaven as a long picnic with the stars at San Simeon. It became the prototype for innumerable memorial gardens elsewhere, but no other had the drawing power of such occupants as Rudolph Valentino and Jean Harlow.

Nor did any other industry more firmly associate images of health, youth, and beauty with the place called California than the movies. Hollywood promotion created a pantheon of gods named Gable, Monroe, Garland, and Cooper. It drew, and continues to draw, thousands of young people hoping to achieve similar immortality, or at least to land a bit part in a television commercial.

Promotional committees and chambers of commerce tirelessly advertised the state as one immense spa. An article of 1901 promoting the Kern River oil fields, for example, claimed that Bakersfield's "location and environment are as thoroughly wholesome as were the slopes of Berkeley in their most charming days."[3] Such enthusiasm produced a strange irony, for those suffering tuberculosis and other chronic ills flocked to California in search of miracle cures while the elderly came in pursuit of rejuvenation and ice-free sidewalks. Pensioners bought bungalows by the mile in Los Angeles, or rented apartments or rooms, while wealthy retirees built villas for their sunset years in Pasadena and Montecito. Sanitariums flourished. For all its imagined youth, Los Angeles had one of the highest age medians in the nation, and by 1900, California could boast more doctors per capita than any other state.

Yet despite the hype, enough truth remained to continue drawing settlers west. California's dry air *did* cure some, and the mild climate along the coast allowed for a degree of outdoor life impossible in most of the rest of the country. Letters to the folks back home—particularly around 1915, when the state had fewer than 3 million people and an electric infrastructure built to accommodate millions more—often expressed a joy in the conditions of life found in a place that was still relatively uncontaminated by industrial and agribusiness wastes. When Robinson and Una Jeffers first saw Carmel in 1914, they knew they had come to their appointed place: "Men were riding after cattle, or plowing the headland, hovered by white sea-gulls, as they have for thousands of years, and will for thousands of years to come."[4] It was, Jeffers later recalled, like Homer's Ithaca then, and he vowed to express that permanence in his verse and in his hand-built stone house; his poetry, however, grew steadily darker as he watched that permanence give way to constant change.

California's lack of coal had proved a blessing, for though it handicapped industry, the state's streams and air remained relatively clean. It was a good place to raise children, *Sunset* endlessly reminded its readers: "They run about in the open air all the year around, and the fat, rosy cheeks and sturdy limbs of the little rogues one meets everywhere tell their own tale of health and happiness."[5]

Sunset did not cover the slums and ghettos of California's growing cities, where disease flourished as prolifically as in less-favored lands. When bubonic plague appeared in San Francisco's Chinatown in 1900, a popular local magazine proposed that anyone spreading the news should be tarred, feathered, and run out of town on a rail. Afraid that fear of the disease would hurt the tourist trade or even place the city under quarantine, the mayor suppressed health reports and vital statistics. The plague spread because of such efforts at damage control, and only a concerted campaign by the U.S. surgeon general succeeded in eradicating the disease as its presence in the city became undeniable.

And illness was not confined to cities. It accompanied poverty and malnutrition into rural California, hidden by promotion that depicted farmers as hardy yeomen or gentleman citrus growers. Even so shrewd a writer as Mary Austin perpetuated the Arcadian myth when she wrote in 1915 of agricultural labor "pass[ing] up and down

Venice Reconstituted, *mural by Rip Cronk, Muscle Beach, Venice, 1989*

the [Central Valley] in 'free companies,' working, eating, and as often as not sleeping in the open. During the brief season of the rains it is housed in packing sheds and preserve factories, but for the greater part of the year the human laborer is as much a part of the great outdoor pageant as the woodpecker or the ant." Life lived so close to nature, concluded Austin, elevated the plane of human existence, so that "one would expect the art of the West to be strongly religious in its implications."[6]

Twenty years later, Dorothea Lange found Mrs. Florence Owens starving with her children in a peapickers' camp outside of Nipomo and depicted her as a modern Madonna in her photograph entitled "Migrant Mother." Her camera also caught the gaunt faces of tubercular fathers, the angular bodies of young girls prematurely old, the bent backs of Filipino, black, and Mexican field hands hoeing and weeding the endless fields that were not their own. She endowed such people with the austere dignity of Renaissance altarpieces. Their rag and tar-paper shanties recalled the manger; a corpse left mysteriously in a simple church doorway showed the way of all flesh.

Having revealed to all what few wanted to see or to believe about the Golden State, Lange's photographs did much to spur on New Deal projects to improve the lot of Americans in general and Californians in particular. Works Progress Administration and Civilian Conservation Corps programs helped many to get through the Depression, while Federal Housing Administration loans kick-started home building in the late 1930s. State and federal relief programs provided a few model workers' camps whose sanitary facilities helped lessen disease among migrant farm workers.

Without knowing it, Farm Security Administration photographers were documenting a way of farming that would be radically altered by chemical research forced by the war. In the decades after the armistice, the "free companies" of agricultural workers, the mi-

grant mothers and their children, and those living near the fields all would be exposed to a growing arsenal of substances used to kill insects and weeds and increase crop yield. Few listened to their complaints of sickness. Crop dusters tended to suffer from cancers, chronic fatigue, and nerve disorders; crashes were frequent. Any connection, the chemical companies assured the public and its clients, was purely coincidental, for the compounds had been thoroughly tested and were harmless to humans when used as directed. One farmer would leave the windows to his house open when the dusters went over; the powder, he said, killed the spiders.[7]

In 1962 a marine biologist put an end to such complacency. Alarmed by the mounting evidence of wildlife dieoffs and habitat destruction caused by chemicals such as DDT, Rachel Carson felt compelled to write something to alert the public. Few other writers could have explained the issues to a broad audience with such clarity and urgency. *Silent Spring* built a damning case upon dozens of tragedies and fiascoes, interspersed with clear explanations of how chemicals work and of their unforeseen consequences.

Chemicals sold as pesticides and herbicides, Carson insisted, should more properly be called *biocides,* for they were seldom as selective as their makers claimed; neither were they used with the care recommended. Since many had evolved from nerve gases developed for wartime use, they were easily absorbed through the skin. Some caused acute symptoms leading to violent sickness and speedy death. Many others, however, worked more insidiously, manifesting themselves only in chronic illness, cancers, or damaged immune systems. Some of them scrambled genetic codes, producing deformities in embryos. In fast-reproducing insects and disease organisms, they had the potential for creating new forms of life.

Carson intended a broader assault than on pesticides alone. Her profound love of the order, permanence, and beauty of the Crea-

Acid fog, Merced, 1986

Home surrounded by pesticide-laden fields,
San Joaquin Valley, 1988

tion had been shaken by the implications of atomic science, by the wholesale release of radioactivity, and by the assurances issued by its practitioners. *Silent Spring* cast doubt on both the objectivity and the omniscience of her fellow scientists at the peak of their prestige. Within a few years, she said, humanity had launched an uncontrolled experiment on itself and every other form of life with which it shared the planet. Carson expected a reaction commensurate with the boldness of her heresy, and she got it.

Silent Spring touched off a firestorm of controversy, especially in California, whose agricultural industry used 10 percent of the world's pesticides and whose petrochemical companies had a vested interest in their sale. According to the industry's spokesmen, Carson was no longer a reputable scientist but a bantamweight, a Luddite willing to turn the world over to insects and disease, the dupe of sinister and alien forces, and most of all, a hysterical woman. Attacks against her intensified as her book became an international bestseller. She defended herself as best she could while cancer sapped her strength. In the spring of 1964 she died, too soon to know that *Silent Spring* would be regarded by many as the fountainhead of a worldwide movement to protect the environment.

Carson provided her critics with a favored target in the eloquent 679-word prologue, which she called "A Fable for Tomorrow." It was, they insisted, science fiction, or mere allegory. She herself admitted she did not know of any place afflicted by all the misfortunes she described, but "the imagined tragedy may easily become a stark reality we all shall know." Twenty years later, that tomorrow became my today when I drove down a dirt road in Merced County into Kesterson National Wildlife Refuge.

"A strange blight crept over the area and everything began to change," she had written, as if foreseeing Kesterson. "The cattle and sheep sickened and died. Everywhere was a shadow of death. The farmers spoke of much illness among their families. In the town the doctors had become more and more puzzled by new kinds of sickness appearing among their patients." There was a strange stillness in both the fable and the marsh at Merced. "The few birds seen anywhere were moribund; they trembled violently and could not fly," wrote Carson. The Freitas family, whose children were sick, watched thousands of coots from the refuge die in their fields. The water from my motel tap tasted oily and the coffee made with it was vile. "Even the streams were now lifeless," Carson said. "Anglers no longer visited them, for all the fish had died." Jim and Karen Claus's kids brought in dead clams, and reported no frogs in the drainage canals.[8]

In the case of Kesterson, the chief culprit turned out to be selenium leached from bad soils on the west side of the valley by irrigation water, but as I worked on the story for a San Francisco television station, I came to realize that I had come to a mining region

billed as a farming valley. *Everything* was coming down the drainage canal from the Westlands fields to the south, hopelessly gumming up expensive filters at a pilot water purification plant built by the state. Throughout the San Joaquin, and in other California farming valleys, Carson's fable no longer seemed so fabulous, but few wanted publicity about what was happening.

Cancers striking children in the towns of Earlimart, Fowler, and McFarland baffled doctors. Babies, like the bird chicks at Kesterson, were born with grotesque deformities. Ground fogs trapped chemicals while windstorms spread them. Fresno became the asthma capital of California, its children carrying inhalers to school and its clinics filled with gasping farmhands. Plumes of pesticides moved underground, contaminating thousands of wells with chemicals that were supposed to stay in the root zones and break down rapidly into harmless components. Many residents of the farming valleys drew their drinking water from those wells.

A state study in 1995 found the highest rates of birth defects were occurring along the Mexico-California border, where the New River claims the distinction of being the filthiest stream in the nation. Picking up the untreated sewage, landfill leachate, and industrial wastes from the Mexican boomtown of Mexicali, the New River swings north to receive the salt, selenium, and pesticides running off the fields of the Imperial Valley in the United States. It dead-ends in the Salton Sea, a stinking reddish-brown sump rapidly growing too rancid for even the hardiest ocean fish. By 1996 the sea had become a deathtrap for birds attracted by the great pool in the desert. They died by the thousands. The coordinator of the birth-defect study admitted that her team was stumped by whatever was causing the deformities in that area.[9]

Parents may be freed of the worry of defects and retardation as they find they can no longer bear children. Many pesticides remain

Cancer victim and mother in front
of contaminated town well,
San Joaquin Valley, 1988

inadequately tested as others come onto the market, and few, if any, are tested in combination, let alone in the nearly infinite mixtures possible in reality. When federal officials did combine two commonly used chemicals in 1996, they found that their combination put the body into overdrive making estrogen, a hormone linked with breast cancer and deformed male sex organs. Sperm count in California, as elsewhere in the world, is dropping fast. Men working in pesticide plants near Stockton found themselves sterilized; the Bay Area claims some of the highest rates of breast cancer in the world, though no one knows why.

Those who move out of the cities often do so for the sake of their children. They want to believe that they have given them the clean air and water traditionally associated with the countryside, as do those farmers who still live on their land. What they discover often disturbs them as profoundly as it did Rachel Carson, who ended her introductory fable with "No witchcraft, no enemy action had silenced the rebirth of new life in this stricken world. The people had done it to themselves."

The workers, however, had it done to them. Their jobs assure them the highest rates of work-related illness in the state. Working

Cancer cluster, McFarland, 1988

Polluted New River, Mexican/American border, Calexico, 1989

Terminus of the New River at the polluted Salton Sea, 1989

Aerial view of oil tanks and South Central Los Angeles, 1993

Apartments near refinery, Richmond, 1989

and living with hazardous chemicals is a danger hardly confined to the fields and processing plants, however, for those chemicals must first be made.

Wherever petroleum refineries locate, there you will find toxic hot spots and the vicinity permeated with chemicals. One of the hottest zones in California lies along the Carquinez Strait in Contra Costa County, where news of refinery fires, toxic leaks, spills, and explosions is commonplace.

Toxic products linger on like the active ingredients in old mine tailings. By the time it closed in 1966, for example, the United Heckathorn Company had dumped enough DDT into the Richmond Inner Harbor to make it the most heavily contaminated site in San

Francisco Bay. When the chemical was banned—largely as a result of Rachel Carson's book—Montrose Chemical and others that produced it simply dumped their inventory of two hundred tons into Santa Monica Bay, once one of the richest marine zones in the nation and now one of the most toxic.

About the time that barrels of DDT were sinking to the bottom off the beaches of Los Angeles, the federal government added its own burden of poison to the Gulf of the Farallones, just west of San Francisco. It was there that Atomic Energy Commission contractors discarded at least 47,500 barrels of radioactive waste in shallow waters serving as a nursery for the local fishing industry and the base of the food chain for the Farallones National Marine Sanctuary.

Homes next to refinery, Long Beach, 1989

Polluted schoolyard, Los Angeles, 1989

Top: *Whites Point, where two hundred tons of DDT are buried underwater, Santa Monica Bay, 1989*

Bottom: *Boy holding fish in a bag, Santa Monica Bay, 1989*

The *New York Times* reported the presence of plutonium contamination in the sediments. Governor George Deukmejian axed fish testing in 1983 to allay fears. Much of the material dumped had come from ships exposed to nuclear tests in the South Pacific and sandblasted in a heavily contaminated black neighborhood in southern San Francisco called Hunters Point.

Hunters Point, too, is a legacy of the Cold War, whose long-hidden costs must now be reckoned with. Of seventeen military bases closed in California, the *San Francisco Examiner* reported in 1992, thirteen would cost taxpayers an estimated $260 million to clean up.[10] That would present fiscal problems, since Congress had budgeted just $300 million to clean up *all* U.S. bases.[11] But three years later the *Chronicle* reported that the Navy had estimated it would cost $300 million to clean up its nuclear submarine base at Mare Island alone, and another $200 million for the Alameda Naval Base.[12] Federal money spent on the Cold War had temporarily lifted the California economy like a rising tide, but in the 1990s that tide pulled out, leaving the coast littered with chemical and radioactive crud that no one wanted, or knew what to do with.

Since the kickoff year of the Gold Rush, and in the past fifty years in particular, the Golden State has become quietly but thoroughly intoxicated. Heavy metals, PCBs, organophosphates, radionuclides, and a vast array of other poisons have soused its waters, soil, and air. If California were to be allegorically portrayed on its 150th birthday, it would look nothing like the virgin flourishing in immortal youth. Rather, it would resemble a badly used whore—chemically dependent and disfigured by abuse—who has seen and tried everything.

Many of those toxins have poured into and collected in San Francisco Bay through the vast network of rivers and streams that

Mural of nuclear dump at the Farallones by Gary Graham, Oakland, 1996

converge on the Delta and the Carquinez Strait. If one regarded the bay's health as indicative of the health of the state, reasoned a retired government official named Bill Davoren, then the prognosis did not look good. Davoren's wife, Bess, had long studied the effects of the environment on the health of individuals; their house looked out across the open water at the refinery belt of Contra Costa County. By 1980, up to 70 percent of the fresh water inflow needed to flush the bay and maintain a relatively healthy ecosystem was being diverted upstream by federal and state pumps. In that year,

Davoren formed the Bay Institute to serve as an advocate for the estuary's environmental health, and by extension, the health of those who lived within its tributary area.

The Davorens were only two of many who had come to rediscover the link between a healthy environment and healthy people. Many others have been provoked into action rather than despair by the magnitude of the problems facing the state. California has never, in fact, lacked for courageous individuals driven by imagination and conviction. They live among us today.

Old military dump site, Hunters Point, San Francisco, 1989

Environmental Response

Monitor measuring slow dispersal of toxic wastes, near Salinas, 1988

Bill Davoren, Tiburon, 1996

"Apathy Got Us Hazardous Waste!" sign in Sierra foothills, 1990

Map of toxic sites, Silicon Valley Toxics Coalition, San Jose, 1988. The map depicts the highest concentration of E.P.A. Superfund cleanup sites in the nation.

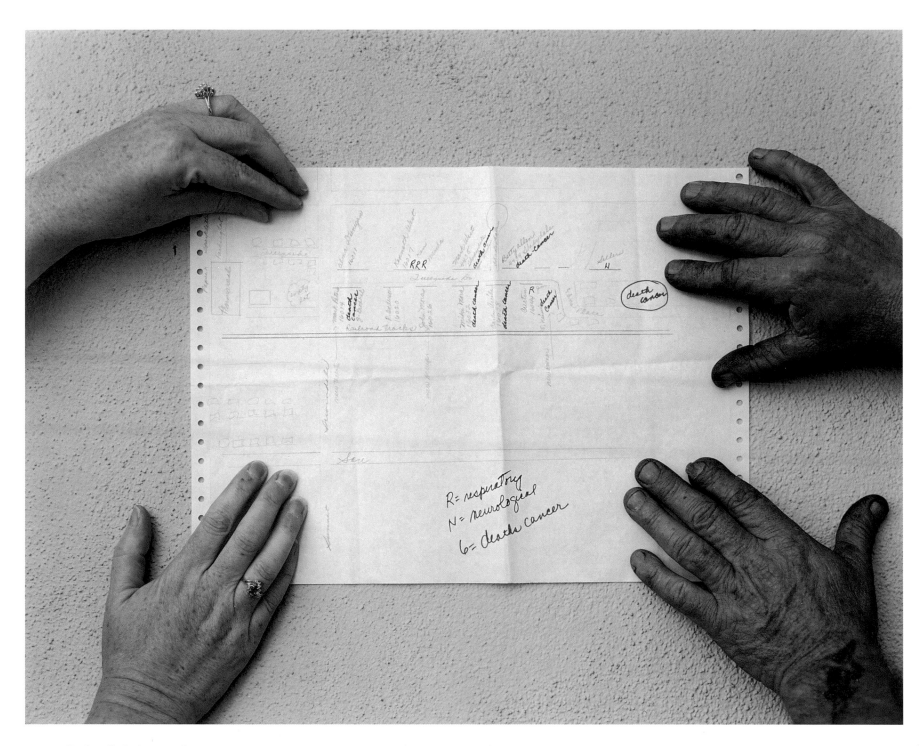

Map of polluted neighborhood, Los Angeles, 1989

Trevor Burrowes (right) worked with residents to grow commercially valuable organic vegetables to break the cycle of poverty in East Palo Alto, 1992.
The town, founded as a utopian colony, ranked in one recent year as the nation's murder capital.

SEVEN: ALTERNATIVE COURSES

If anything has impressed me during my years of reading old newspapers and magazines, it is how materialism has permeated California culture since the Gold Rush. It did so to such a degree that it had to be continually excused by notions of progress and growth as tightly intertwined as the double strands of DNA. Few other values have had a serious chance to challenge moneymaking and spending as the ultimate meaning of human existence. The creation of great fortunes justified the stripping of Lake Tahoe forests and of redwood groves often referred to as God's cathedrals. It permitted the despoliation of magnificent coastlines and rivers by oil wells and factories, the extermination of humans and wildlife, and the poisoning of those who live and work near smelters, refineries, and farmlands. Nothing remained sacred except the right to accumulate wealth; churches and synagogues were razed and cemeteries moved or forgotten when they stood in the way of what some defined as progress. When, in 1913, workmen finished the demolition of a great native shell mound estimated to contain as many as 10,000 skeletons, the *San Francisco Call* perfunctorily mourned that "the sacred burial place of the past ages should give way to city lots, and that

this spot, known to the scientists of the world, is soon to be the commercial center of Richmond's inner harbor activity."[1] The culture that produced that mound had made soil of its wastes; that which replaced it produced enduring toxins called DDT and dieldrin, which it dumped into San Francisco Bay from the same spot.

Alternative voices, however minor, thus carry important messages down to us in the present. What W. H. Auden said of space as World War II began is true of time as well: "Yet dotted everywhere, / Ironic points of light / Flash out wherever the Just / Exchange their messages."[2] I find those ironic points of light throughout history in the voices of people who questioned popular notions of progress and who attempted to light the way down different paths.

Bayard Taylor wrote during the Gold Rush that California would repeat the glories of Greece, but Frederick Law Olmsted, shortly thereafter, lamented how far short of that promise it fell. Throughout his life, Olmsted sought ways to create from the democratic ideals of the American Constitution and the North American continent a civilization that would enlighten the world by its example. Because there existed no terms for what he wished to accomplish, he struggled with himself and with his friends to define it. California helped him put what he himself wished to do into both words and deeds.

He began, in the 1850s, by designing Central Park in Manhattan with architect Calvert Vaux. Both men wished to create more than just a park, however. They called their design "the big art work of the Republic," a commons deliberately open to all on an island already noted for flamboyant excesses of wealth. But before it could be completed, the Civil War tore the republic apart.

The strain involved in setting up the forerunner of the American Red Cross broke Olmsted's health. Accepting a job offer to manage a near-bankrupt mining estate near Mariposa, he shipped out to California in 1864. His two years in the Far West gave Olmsted the time and experience that he needed to clarify for himself what he wanted to accomplish. His writings from that period provide a bonanza of ideas far more valuable in the late twentieth century than the gold that eluded him in the 1860s.[3]

The westward movement was, for Olmsted, no romantic pageant, but a "grand game of assassination" often carried forth by the most savage elements of society.[4] With a few notable exceptions, California and San Francisco exhibited the most extreme case of barbarism masquerading as civilization that he had ever witnessed. Rather than cultivating the land, the invaders were raping it; rather than tolerance, he found an intolerable degree of racism and violence directed at numerous and convenient scapegoats who allowed the newcomers to escape self-reflection.

How should men be judged? he asked himself in his unpublished "Notes on the Pioneer Condition." Certainly not by their material possessions alone: "I come to the conclusion that the highest point on my scale can only be met by the man who possesses a combination of qualities which fit him to serve others and to be served by others in the most intimate, complete and extend[ed] degree imaginable." He called this social contract "communitiveness." Similarly, he defined civility as "an all-embracing relationship based upon the confidence, respect, and interest of each citizen in all and all in each." Such *responsive* relationships formed the basis on which all truly admirable cities and civilizations are built. He found, he said, less of this sense of community in California than in any other body of men he had ever encountered: "And the white men, the Englishmen, the Germans, and other civilized men do not possess [it] often in as high degree as the Mexicans, Chinese and negroes."[5]

The violence Anglos directed against those they deemed inferior was reflected in a similar violence toward a land deserving of care. From Mariposa, Olmsted and his family rode their horses into a granite-walled Eden recently discovered by army scouts in pursuit of Indians. They walked through the parklike meadows of the Yosemite Valley and the giant trees near its gateway which, he had earlier told his wife, were like "distinguished strangers who have come down to us from another world."[6] Given the prevailing trend of private exploitation, Olmsted feared for what might befall both the valley and the trees. When asked by the governor to make suggestions for the newly discovered wonders, Olmsted wrote a remarkable report, published in the summer of 1865.

The valley and the trees, he said, belonged to all people and should be made a commons like Central Park. His recommendation was, according to the editors of his papers, not only "the first comprehensive statement on the preservation of natural scenery in America"; it also laid the foundation for a system of national parks now emulated around the world.[7]

Olmsted went so far as to propose elsewhere that lands wrecked by mining should be reclaimed afterwards, and that English-style landscapes, requiring immense amounts of water, were inappropriate and wasteful in arid lands like California. Such suggestions were far too radical for his time, but by the time he left in October 1865 to resume work on Central Park and other projects, he had planted ideas that would germinate decades later.

Three years after Olmsted left, a long-bearded Scotsman prone to mystical euphoria arrived in San Francisco and immediately departed to see Yosemite and the Sierra Nevada. Far more concerned with wilderness than Olmsted, John Muir found personal salvation in the mountains. Muir would be instrumental, through his writing, in implementing Olmsted's idea of a national park for Yosemite. He alerted a broad public to the splendors they had inherited and were so rapidly wrecking, and in 1892 he joined with like-minded friends in San Francisco to form one of the earliest conservation organizations, the Sierra Club. Among the club's goals was "to enlist the support and cooperation of the people and the government in preserving the forests and other natural features of the Sierra Nevada." [8]

Others protested at the same time against the widespread racism that had already eliminated some people and relegated others to ghettos and serfdom. Helen Hunt Jackson's *A Century of Dishonor* appeared as early as 1881, indicting the federal government for its injustice toward American Indians. The book earned her a commission from the Department of the Interior to write an official report on the needs of California natives, a report that was promptly pigeonholed and forgotten. Her 1884 bestseller *Ramona,* rather than having the intended effect of eliciting sympathy for the natives, kicked off the Mission Revival in architecture and an enduring nostalgia for the graciously imaginary days of the Spanish dons.

Josiah Royce, too, deplored the conflict between the "vast plan of the country," its "noble frankness," and the willful self-delusions of the people who lived there. Having grown up in Grass Valley and attended the state university at Berkeley, Royce jumped at an offer

to teach at Harvard. From there, the precocious philosopher published a critical history in 1886 called *California.* "All this tale is one of disgrace to our people," he said of the racism that afflicted his state as thoroughly as it did the South. [9] An anonymous reviewer predictably savaged the book in the *Overland Monthly,* calling it immature and irreverent. Royce had expected such treatment from a literary magazine whose motto was "Devoted to the Development of the Country," but the criticism stung him nonetheless.

Those Californians whom Olmsted would have found most genuinely civilized often lived not in the cultural capital of San Francisco but in small country towns. A remarkable family in Ukiah took a keen interest in the local Pomo Indians, collecting their artifacts and recording their stories. Helen Carpenter possessed a sense of common humanity that expressed itself in a stream of articles championing the rights of Indians. Her 1893 account of the kidnapping and enslavement of native children, published in the *Overland Monthly,* has lost little of its power to outrage a century later. Her daughter, Grace Hudson, became famous for her sympathetic oil portraits and drawings of the Pomos.

In attempting to civilize the state, women played a major role in the conservation movement as well as in humanitarian activities and town planning. Motivated by a deep Christian ethic, Annie Bidwell protected Indians on her Chico ranch, while Donaldina Cameron worked in San Francisco's Chinatown to save girls from white slavery. Many other women established settlement houses and libraries to better integrate poor immigrants into America; the parks and street trees that grace many of California's pleasanter towns are often the forgotten legacy of women's improvement clubs. Founded largely by university wives in 1898, the Hillside Club persuaded the town of Berkeley to give up the grid plan when it reached the

Lucy Thompson, Yurok, c. 1915 (collection of Peter E. Palmquist)

hills. Its stated goal was to save as much of the natural landscape as possible and to enhance it by human design. For those women, a town first had to be beautiful in order to earn the love necessary to make it more so. Inspired by Berkeley's success, Mrs. Lovell White founded the Outdoor Art Club in Mill Valley, from which she conducted a national campaign that collected 1.4 million signatures to save the Calaveras Big Trees from logging. In 1916 a Yurok woman named Lucy Thompson published an account of her people and their decimation entitled *To the American Indian.* Oakland journalist and self-taught historian Delilah L. Beasley fought for civil rights; meticulously collecting facts, she told a parallel but unknown history of the West in her 1919 book, *Negro Trail Blazers of California.*

California abounded in the utopian experiments of those who tried to leave the mainstream and build entirely new societies. One such was founded on the alkali shores of Tulare Lake by a man who could have been one of Beasley's heroes, Colonel Allen Allensworth. Now a state park, Allensworth was the only town in California settled and governed entirely by African Americans. Other experiments include the more or less communist communities at Icaria Speranza, Llano del Rio, and Kaweah, as well as numerous back-to-the-land colonies such as Runnymede and San Ysidro.

These are but a few of the individuals and groups who, in their own ways, attempted to civilize California but whose stories are far less known than celebrities such as the railroad magnates and the silver kings. Their numbers would multiply exponentially after 1945.

The first rumble came from San Francisco early in 1947, when newspaper columnist Herb Caen announced that the city planned to junk the last of its cable cars. According to a promotion issued to ready citizens for the change in their public transit system, the

Tulare County Free Library, Colonel Allensworth State Historic Park, San Joaquin Valley, 1995

Llano del Rio, near Los Angeles, 1993

picturesque but obsolete relics of the Victorian age would give way to clean, comfortable, and efficient diesel buses. City politicians, bureaucrats, and promoters did not anticipate that a determined and well-connected clubwoman named Mrs. Frieda Klussmann would derail their plans.

Klussmann was never one to accept a reflexive "That's progress" as synonymous with the inevitable. She rallied friends and celebrities to oppose the liquidation of the world's last cable railway system, marshaling figures in public hearings to disprove her opposition's insistence that buses were, in fact, cheaper to run on San Francisco's city streets. She challenged the city's consultant as an auto industry shill who had recently destroyed Seattle's cable system. At first dismissed as a meddlesome woman, Klussmann began to be taken more seriously after she masterminded the defeat of pro-bus mayor Roger Lapham. Ultimately, she succeeded in saving half of the existing cable car system and having it declared a National Historic Landmark in 1964. By the time of her death in 1986, she was revered as "the Cable Car Lady."

Post office, Kaweah, 1994

Klussmann's quixotic campaign was only the first in a movement questioning the received wisdom of infinite growth and accelerating change. Just before Christmas in 1955, two thousand angry San Franciscans met startled and unprepared engineers from the State Division of Highways at Lincoln High School to demand information. They had heard that the Highway Division was preparing to launch a massive freeway-building program throughout the city that would decimate neighborhoods, tear through Golden Gate Park, and wall the waterfront from the bay. The meeting marked the beginning of the freeway revolt that brought together all San Francisco neighborhoods, often in alliance with citizens of Marin and aided by the tireless Mrs. Klussmann. The revolt ultimately terminated most of San Francisco's projected freeways, providing the inspiration needed by activists in New Orleans, Boston, and other major cities.

At the same time that some were challenging concrete, others were questioning nuclear fallout and reactors. A growing number of citizens remained unconvinced by official assurances that radio-

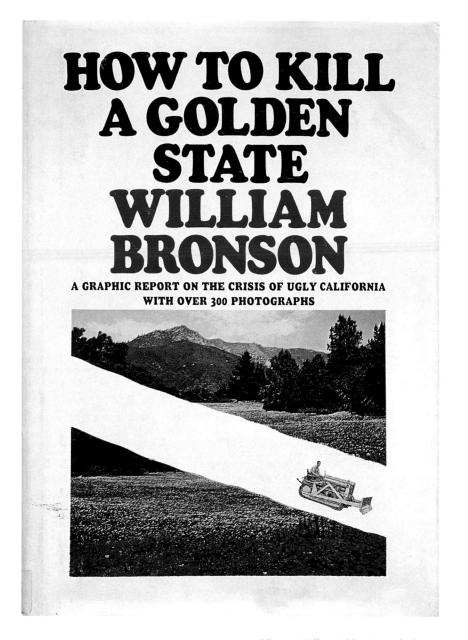

HOW TO KILL A GOLDEN STATE
WILLIAM BRONSON

A GRAPHIC REPORT ON THE CRISIS OF UGLY CALIFORNIA WITH OVER 300 PHOTOGRAPHS

How to Kill a Golden State, *book cover*

activity showered upon the world by atmospheric tests posed little or no danger to public health. Such opposition required courage, for given Cold War hysteria and the immensely lucrative industries growing around the arms race, those who protested ran the risk of being investigated or blacklisted as subversives.

Nonetheless, when the Pacific Gas & Electric Company announced its plans to build an "atomic park" at Bodega Bay north of San Francisco in 1958, a small group of activists organized to challenge the necessary permit. The utility had, they pointed out, sited its reactor virtually on top of the San Andreas rift zone on heavily sheared granite; the company replied that its engineers were up to the challenge. A rising tide of local and national opposition eventually forced PG&E to cancel construction on the reactor in 1964. The site became a state park, and the spot intended for the reactor foundation is now a wildlife marsh.

The 1960s saw an avalanche of opposition and questioning, which gained power and legitimacy with the publication of Rachel Carson's *Silent Spring*. Radical changes in the San Francisco skyline and quality of life spawned the highrise revolt. At the same time, opposition grew throughout the Bay Area to more freeways and bridges, as well as to the wholesale destruction of architectural landmarks. Books and periodicals called attention to the rapidly deteriorating state of California's environment: Raymond Dasmann's *Destruction of California* (1965); Richard G. Lilliard's *Eden in Jeopardy* (1966), which focused on southern California; and William Bronson's *How to Kill a Golden State* (1968). The group California Tomorrow published a smart and gutsy little magazine from 1965 to 1982 called *Cry California*, which remains to this day a fountain of imaginative solutions to California's growing problems. Its insistence that California have a state land-use plan to guide its growth and preserve prime farmlands has been consistently ignored by successive legislatures and governors.

Perhaps the single most important campaign, however, was the battle to save the very feature that gave the Bay Area its name. Ever since John Parrott had watched in "grim satisfaction" as a steam paddy filled the harbor to make room for "stately palaces of trade," developers had eyed the bay as potential real estate. A promoter named John Reber hawked a perennial scheme to dam the north and south ends of the bay to create what he optimistically described as freshwater lakes. The lakes would then, he said, trigger the kind of development that would gradually lead to their filling. In 1947, Reber told a U.S. Senate subcommittee: "This whole bay is too big. Some day a hundred years from now it will be half that big." [10]

According to an Army Corps of Engineers study released in 1959, Reber's casual estimate wasn't nearly ambitious enough. At the rate at which the bay was then being filled, it wouldn't take nearly a century before it was much less than half the size it had been when he made his prediction. The report showed that the bay had already shrunk by almost a third from its original extent at the beginning of the Gold Rush. It was well on its way to becoming a river.

In 1960 three influential faculty wives at the University of California—Catherine Kerr, Sylvia McLaughlin, and Esther Gulick—organized their friends and associates to stop the filling. They were particularly concerned about plans announced by the Crocker Land Company and associated developers to decapitate Mount San Bruno south of San Francisco for the material needed to fill much of the south bay, while the city of Berkeley announced its intention to fill more than three square miles along its waterfront. The women's Save San Francisco Bay Association found that cities and developers throughout the Bay Area were independently developing their

Founders of Save San Francisco Bay Association, Oakland, 1987. Left to right: *Sylvia McLaughlin, Catherine Kerr, and Esther Gulick (photo by Richard Barnes)*

own ambitious plans to expand into open water. A laborious campaign led to the creation, in 1965, of a temporary regional agency called the San Francisco Bay Conservation Study Commission. Four years later, the state legislature made the Bay Conservation and Development Commission a permanent agency and gave it the power to significantly direct growth in the public interest. The BCDC not only halted the bay's shrinkage, but actually reversed it, creating new marshes from diked baylands and opening miles of shoreline previously off limits to the public.

A multi-county agency with that kind of power was something new in California. With the example of the BCDC as a model, Californians in 1972 passed Proposition 20, which created the California Coastal Zone Commission. That agency has quietly preserved much of what remains of one of the nation's most spectacular coastlines. At the same time, the federal government's Clean Water and Clean Air Acts succeeded in greatly reducing visible pollution.

Most of these movements were, to some extent, led by Brahmin conservationists in the Sierra Club. Muir's club had long been run by upper-class professionals, but that began to change in the 1960s and 1970s when, under the activist leadership of David Brower, it greatly expanded its membership and range of concerns, becoming one of the largest and most effective conservation organizations in the world, while at the same time retaining an unusually decentralized structure. Many other environmental organizations sprang up in response to specific concerns, often fed by grassroots activists and veterans of the '60s counterculture.

Among the most important of the special-interest groups was the Mono Lake Committee, which initially came together over its founders' love for a mysterious desert lake lying at the foot of the Sierra just east of Yosemite National Park. The Los Angeles Department of Water and Power, after first drying up Owens Lake far to the south, had extended its aqueduct into the Mono Basin in its relentless quest for new sources of water. The extension intercepted most of the creeks that fed Mono Lake from the Sierra snowpack. Deprived of virtually its entire inflow, the lake was rapidly shrinking when, in the mid-1970s, a group of biologists turned from studying the lake to saving it. They were led by a charismatic birdwatcher named David Gaines, whose hero was John Muir. Gaines gave slideshows throughout California to alert people to the little-known lake and its imminent peril.

A backpacking legal scholar provided the needed ammunition. Tim Such proposed that Mono Lake was covered by an ancient but largely unenforced doctrine called the public trust, which holds that the lake is, in fact, a commons protected by the people's representative—the State of California. No one had given Los Angeles permission to destroy a body of water nearly 350 miles from the city. The San Francisco law firm of Morrison & Foerster, in 1979, found Such's idea intriguing enough to take the case *pro bono publico.* On February 17, 1983, the California Supreme Court agreed, ruling that Los Angeles had no right to take the lake.

The Supreme Court ruling was only the beginning of a tortuous legal and administrative battle that dragged on for over eleven more years until, in September of 1994, the city agreed to relinquish the streams. As snowmelt once more coursed down the long-dry channels into the lake, Mono stopped shrinking and began to rise dramatically, covering alkali-crusted mudflats. Fresh water pulled the lake back from a degree of salinity nearly fatal to the ecosystem it had once supported. The basin's vital signs quickened as willows once again greened its feeder streams. Flycasters and migrating birds have returned every year in greater abundance, and tourists flock to watch a miraculous resurrection.

The true importance of the Supreme Court's 1983 ruling lay in

Tufa and clouds, Mono Lake, 1986

Aurora Castillo, founder of Mothers of East L.A., Los Angeles, 1995

its establishment of a precedent as important as Judge Sawyer's 1884 decision against the hydraulic mines; the public trust covered environmental values that could be used as a counterweight to the piecemeal destruction of California that had prevailed since the Gold Rush.

Increasingly, many activists have organized not so much around aesthetics as around issues of health and crime, finding in the sickening of the environment the causes for illnesses in their own families and communities. In this respect, the civil rights movement has begun to converge with the environmental movement, further broadening its base and changing its complexion.

As early as 1870, well-to-do residents of Oakland fought back a smelter that threatened the health of their families and real estate. More than a century later, the poor are refusing to take the waste products given them by others. They call such dumping toxic racism; their impertinence has increasingly caused headaches for those charged with getting rid of the toxic by-products of inequitable prosperity.

The barrio of East Los Angeles has long served as just such a dumping ground. A modest residential district whose broad streets are lined with tamale stands and check-cashing stores, the neighborhood lies next to the rust belt of the Los Angeles River. The late Aurora Castillo, a fourth-generation Mexican American deeply committed to her community, its children, and her church, organized and effectively led the group known as Mothers of East Los Angeles in successfully blocking a toxic waste incinerator, a hazardous waste storage facility, and the region's eighth prison. A woman of as much dignity as conviction, she was named in 1995 a recipient of the Goldman Environmental Prize. In her accep-

tance speech, *La Doña*, as she was respectfully known in her neighborhood, told an international audience that *all* people are entitled to clean air, clean water, and pure food, regardless of their race or class.

That has been the message of a growing number of similar grassroots organizations. In Richmond, the West County Toxics Coalition operates out of a storefront in a town devastated by toxic releases and capital flight. The coalition collects information on residents who suffer from diseases ranging from severe asthma to cancer. North Richmond, says WCTC director Henry Clark, is "not a place anyone with any other choice would choose to live," and so he has chosen to make it better by working for cleanup and restitution.[11] Similarly, residents of the largely Mexican American town of Kettleman City, in central California, blocked a proposed incinerator designed to burn the most toxic wastes. Near the Arizona border, the five Colorado River Indian tribes have joined with environmentalists to fight federal plans for a nuclear waste dump in Ward Valley, uncomfortably close to the Colorado River.

Opposition to the wreck of California has also manifested itself in a growing number of preserves designed to save what little remains of the original landscape, as well as ambitious plans to restore to health what has been degraded. The former includes a little-known system of outdoor "museums" maintained by the non-profit Nature Conservancy, the University of California, and the California State University system. Their holdings range from the most unassuming native grasslands and vernal pools in the Central Valley to a spectacular granite mountain range in the Mojave Desert. More ambitiously, volunteers working with the Nature Conservancy and allied groups are restoring an extensive oak woodlands

The West County Toxics Coalition, Richmond, 1996

California State University System's Desert Studies Center, Zzyzx, 1992

on the Cosumnes River between Sacramento and Stockton and as much as 28,000 acres of riparian forests and prairies at the Llano Seco Ranch on the upper Sacramento River.

Water has drawn many citizens together who organize to rehabilitate degraded streams. Without knowing it, they are rediscovering Frederick Law Olmsted and Werner Hegemann's suggestions to build communities around local watercourses. It is therefore appropriate that the movement to save urban streams began precisely where both men made their proposals—in Oakland and Berkeley.

Begun largely as the vision of middle-class environmentalists, the creek restoration movement has now been adopted by all classes and become a national movement. The goal of many—hopeless as it may often seem in light of the deplorable condition of most urban streams—is to see the creeks once again support salmon runs.

In 1969, well-to-do citizens of Marin lay down in front of bulldozers to block plans by the Army Corps of Engineers to turn Corte Madera Creek into yet another of its standard-issue concrete flood-control channels. In the 1980s, mothers in north Richmond living

Urban creek restoration and Dave Rosgen, Wildcat Creek, Berkeley, 1993

not far from Henry Clark's storefront operation resisted a similar plan for their own Wildcat Creek. With the aid of stream restorationists Luna Leopold and Ann Riley at the University of California, they persuaded the Corps to develop an innovative "soft" flood-control project that included a streamside greenbelt and educational center for their children at Verdi Elementary School. Other activists working in the hills have made common cause with those living in the flats to restore the health of the stream. The healing of Wildcat Creek, which courses past the refineries that line the bay and through one of the region's poorest neighborhoods, provides others with an example of what can be accomplished by human de-

sign and action; if salmon can return to such a creek, then almost anything is possible.

On a far grander scale, the Friends of the Los Angeles River (FOLAR) has organized around the stream that William Mulholland once loved in its natural state. In a city so divided along racial and economic lines, FOLAR envisions the river as a means of bringing citizens together rather than separating them, as it has for so long. Among the most degraded streams in the state, the Los Angeles River seems to many irredeemably lost, but FOLAR co-founder Lewis MacAdams takes the long view, describing his vision as "a forty-year art work," which drives him and his allies to muster support for their vision.[12]

Where some gather around water, others focus on one of California's most frequently touted but flagrantly abused assets—its soil. Such mistreatment deeply disturbed Professor Hans Jenny, an earth scientist at the University of California who saw soil not simply as a medium for holding crops upright but as a living skin, furred with plants and deserving the greatest respect and care. Interviewed in 1984 near the end of his life, Jenny spoke of soil as a thing of beauty, sensuality, and wonder, regretting the disinterest and contempt with which so many people treat it. "Perhaps as long as supermarkets are well stocked with food, the city dweller does not look beyond," he mused, further observing that when one attempted to find the boundary between a root and a healthy soil under an electron microscope, one could not distinguish between them. In the realization of such integrity, Jenny said, soil science approached for him the threshold of religion and mysticism.[13]

Psychologists, gardeners, and those devoted to farming have long known that working with healthy soil has a therapeutic effect. San Francisco's League of Urban Gardeners finds vacant city lots from which it creates community gardens. As in many other cities with

Lewis MacAdams and the Los Angeles River,
Los Angeles, 1995

such programs, SLUG has found it must maintain a long waiting list for the many apartment dwellers eager to have even the smallest plot of ground, and that communities grow around gardens as they do around creeks.

Ruth Brinker, founder of a project called Open Hand, which provides meals to people with AIDS, has initiated another project, called Fresh Start Gardens, designed to put homeless people to work growing high-priced organic vegetables for the many restau-

rants that have followed the example of Alice Waters's Chez Panisse in Berkeley. Brinker, like Waters, believes that such a project can help people who have lost all hope to reclaim their lives. The same goal motivates Cathrine Sneed, who works with prisoners at San Francisco's city jail to grow organic vegetables in greenhouses south of the city. Sneed has witnessed just the kind of rehabilitation in her workers that Brinker hopes to accomplish at her urban farms. In north Oakland, Pat Nagle and Sharon Joyer helped organize a

*Saint Mary's Urban Youth Farm, a project of the San Francisco League
of Urban Gardeners (SLUG), San Francisco (diptych), 1996*

Ruth Brinker, Fresh Start Gardens, San Francisco, 1996

community garden on a long-disused backyard donated by neighborhood elder Lillie Luckett. The garden, said Nagle, is a means of teaching children about cooperation, energy flow, and interdependence. In the drug-torn ghetto of East Palo Alto, activist Trevor Burrowes has worked to reclaim the utopian ideal of the town's founder, who promised settlers an "acre of land and independence." Burrowes, too, sees intensive farming as a way for the town's residents to break out of the cycle of poverty, dependence, and violence.

All of these people, and the many more working quietly throughout the state and federal governments to heal the land, possess the quality that Olmsted called communitiveness. Others, such as Michael Abelman at his Fairview Gardens in Goleta, Gloria and Steve Decater at their community-supported farm in Covelo, and Fred Smeds in the San Joaquin Valley, see organic farming not only as a healthier way to live but also as a means of reestablishing a lost sense of responsibility between the city and the land that sustains it.

Cathrine Sneed, San Francisco Jail Garden Project, San Bruno, 1996

Lillie Luckett Community Garden, Oakland, 1996

Such efforts often seem minuscule in light of the enormous threats facing California. Short-sightedness has been one of the state's most enduring features and abundant exports. But whenever I look across San Francisco Bay's still-open waters at the stretch of green and gold headlands flanking the Golden Gate, I reflect on the past and take heart.

It was there, following the war, that the State Division of Highways planned to build a second bridge and force a freeway through the coastal hills. The freeway would have followed the route of the San Andreas fault and opened it to full-bore development. Marincello, a proposed city of fifty sixteen-story highrises in the hills just north of the bridge, was only a prelude for what was to follow on the north coast. The work of hundreds of activists successfully blocked that proposal and created in its place the Point Reyes National Seashore and the Golden Gate National Recreation Area, a more than 120,000-acre preserve of open space wrapping around the Gulf of the Farallones. No other city in the world possesses a commons as splendid as these parks, or a group of citizens more deserving of gratitude for a vision realized. It is a lesson for all who would despair at the claims of those championing a progress they claim is inevitable and nonnegotiable.

California has long served as the nation's rift zone between fantasy and reality. Along that tense fissure, creativity and commitment have welled up, together with the more newsworthy forces of violence and destruction. Those who have come to this remarkable strip of land along the Pacific are learning that they can no longer rely on the promises made by promoters to draw them here. They must learn to understand and appreciate, as Olmsted wrote in 1864, the fixed qualities of the place if they are to build something worth calling a civilization upon it. Only by treating the land—

Statue of Philip Burton, United States Representative
primarily responsible for creating the Golden Gate
National Recreation Area, 1996

the skin of its soil, the blood of its streams, and the breath of its sea winds—as worthy of the same love with which we endow those closest to us will California become not simply real estate, but home.

Gerbode Valley, site of defeated Marincello development, Golden Gate National Recreation Area (diptych), 1996

Bank covered in netting and new grasses, Lake Tahoe, 1993

Pipe used in restoration efforts, Mattole River, 1995

Above: *Bay Area environmentalists, 1996: George Collins (right) was a partner in Conservation Associates, one of the nation's first land trusts, and past president of the Nature Conservancy. His son Josh is an environmental scientist at the San Francisco Estuary Institute.*

Opposite: *Friends of the Urban Forest's tree planting, Islais Creek, Bayview District, San Francisco, 1993*

Gray Brechin on bridge, Grizzly Island Wildlife Area, San Francisco Bay Estuary, 1995

Canal and boat, San Francisco Bay National Wildlife Refuge, 1995

Looking into the Tule Elk State Reserve, near Bakersfield, 1995

Hills and grass at sunset, Carrizo Plain, 1995

Scientists discussing the demise and restoration of California's salmon near the Sacramento River, 1997

Preface

1. From "Sinaloa Cowboys," copyright © 1995 Bruce Springsteen (ASCAP). All rights reserved. Lyrics reprinted by permission.

2. Quotes are from J. S. Holliday, *The World Rushed In: The California Gold Rush Experience* (New York: Simon and Schuster, 1981), pp. 369, 401, and 458.

3. Joan Didion, *Slouching Towards Bethlehem* (New York: Simon and Schuster, 1968), p. 176.

Chapter One

1. John Muir, "The Bee Pastures," in *The Mountains of California* (Garden City, N.Y.: Anchor Books, 1961), pp. 259–89.

2. Mayfield's story is told in *Indian Summer: Traditional Life among the Choinumne Indians of California's San Joaquin Valley* (Berkeley: Heyday Books and California Historical Society, 1993).

3. J. W. A. Wright, "The Distant Sierra," *Mining and Scientific Press*, November 3, 1883, p. 286.

4. Muir, "The Sierra Nevada," in *The Mountains of California*, p. 2.

5. *Bakersfield Republican*, January 20, 1954.

6. "Tulare Lake Dried Up," *San Francisco Call*, August 14, 1898.

7. Stephen Powers, *Tribes of California* (Berkeley: University of California Press, 1976), pp. 404–5.

8. Helen M. Carpenter, "Among the Diggers of Thirty Years Ago," *Overland Monthly* 21, no. 124 (April 1893): pp. 389–99.

9. Van H. Garner, *The Broken Ring: The Destruction of the California Indians* (Tucson: Westernlore Press, 1982), pp. 98–99.

10. Copyright © 1978, 1979, 1991 by Peter Nabokov; foreword copyright © 1991 by Vine Deloria, Jr. Excerpt used by permission of Viking Penguin, a division of Penguin Putnam Inc.

11. Francis J. A. Darr, "Indian Education Applied to the San Carlos Reservation," *Overland Monthly* 5, no. 26 (February 1885): p. 195.

12. Thomas Magee, "Overworked Soils," *Overland Monthly* 1 (October 1868): p. 329.

13. Frank Norris, *The Octopus* (New York: Bantam Books, 1963), p. 198.

Chapter Two

1. Theodora Kroeber, *Ishi in Two Worlds: A Biography of the Last Wild Indian in North America* (Berkeley: University of California Press, 1961), pp. 52–53.

2. Charles Nordhoff, *California: For Health, Pleasure and Residence: A Book for Travellers and Settlers* (Berkeley: Ten Speed Press, 1973 [facsimile of 1873 edition]), p. 188.

3. Samuel Bowles, *Our New West: Records of Travel between the Mississippi River and the Pacific Ocean* (Bowie, Md.: Heritage Books, 1990), pp. 422–23.

4. William L. Merry, "San Francisco Commerce, Past, Present, and Future," *Overland Monthly* 9, no. 64 (April 1888): 373.

5. "The Biggest Mine in California," *San Francisco Chronicle*, October 1, 1899.

6. "Abandoned Mines Continue to Pollute the Sacramento," *San Francisco Chronicle*, June 17, 1992.

7. Tom Knudson, "Mines Foul Sierra Streams," *Sacramento Bee*, June 12, 1991.

8. J. S. Holliday, *The World Rushed In: The California Gold Rush Experience* (New York: Simon and Schuster, 1981), p. 401.

Chapter Three

1. Frank Norris, *The Octopus* (New York: Bantam Books, 1963), p. 198.

2. Robert Lloyd Kelley, *Battling the Inland Sea: American Political Culture, Public Policy, and the Sacramento Valley, 1850–1986* (Berkeley: University of California Press, 1989), p. 303.

3. Charles Nordhoff, *California: For Health, Pleasure and Residence: A Book for Travellers and Settlers* (Berkeley: Ten Speed Press, 1973 [facsimile of 1873 edition]), p. 188.

4. According to the 1987 agricultural census, 1,012 landowners owned more than 15 million acres (nearly half) of private agricultural land in California, a figure little changed from the early 1870s. Compilers of the 1979 *Atlas of California* noted that "it was impossible to map corporate ownership. For whatever reason (unwillingness to admit to the power that possession of land confers, moral or legal problems with taxing bodies, or simple distaste for the public disclosure of private ownership), the major land owners of California have always been opposed to any effort to publicize the size and location of their holdings." Michael W. Donley et al., *Atlas of California* (Culver City: Pacific Book Center, 1979), p. 63.

5. Gerald Haslam, *The Great Central Valley: California's Heartland* (Berkeley: University of California Press, 1993), p. 41.

6. Walter V. Woehlke, "The Great Valley: A Critical Examination of the Golden State's Economic Backbone," *Sunset* 34, no. 2 (February 1915): 290.

7. James Bryce, *The American Commonwealth* (London: Macmillan, 1888), Vol. 2, p. 386.

8. Earle Crowe, *Men of El Tejon* (Los Angeles: W. Ritchie Press, 1957), pp. 142–43.

9. "Opium Culture—A New Branch of Industry," *California Mail Bag*, June 1871, p. xvii; "Culture of the Poppy for Opium," *Mining and Scientific Press*, February 12, 1870, p. 102.

10. *San Francisco Chronicle*, December 31, 1905.

11. David Igler, "When Is a River Not a River? Reclaiming Nature's Disorder in *Lux v. Haggin*," *Environmental History* 1, no. 2 (April 1996), pp. 52–69.

12. Walter V. Woehlke, "The Great Valley," p. 293.

13. Bernard DeVoto, *The Easy Chair* (Boston: Houghton Mifflin, 1955), p. 245.

14. Edgar French, "The Re-Discovery of California," *The World's Work* 18, no. 4 (August 1909): 11899–900.

15. Woehlke, "The San Joaquin," *Sunset* 30, no. 3 (March 1913): 220.

16. *San Francisco Chronicle*, October 19, 1913.

17. Ellen Liebman, *California Farmland: A History of Large Agricultural Landholdings* (Totowa, N.J.: Rowman and Allanhead, 1983), p. 97.

18. Hamilton Candee and Laura King, *The Broken Promise of Reclamation Reform* (San Francisco: Natural Resources Defense Council, October 1987).

19. Charles Wollenberg, "The Last Jeffersonian," paper presented to the Pacific Coast Branch of the American Historical Society, August 1994, Corvallis, Oregon.

20. Joan Zoloth-Dalzell, "Catch 22," *San Francisco Examiner*, August 12, 1992.

21. Susan Ferris, "Fields of Broken Dreams," *San Francisco Examiner*, *Image* magazine, July 18, 1993, p. 12.

22. Dorothea Lange and Paul S. Taylor, *An American Exodus: A Record of Human Erosion* (New York: Reynal and Hitchcock, 1939), p. 147.

23. Robert Collier, "Where the Cattle Once Roamed," *This World, San Francisco Chronicle*, December 20, 1992. See also *Generating Values in California Real Estate in the 90s: The Newhall Fact Book* (Valencia, Calif.: Newhall Land and Farming Company, 1990).

Chapter Four

1. Barbara Donohoe Jostes, *John Parrott, Consul: 1811–1884* (San Francisco, Lawton and Alfred Kennedy, 1972), p. 105.

2. James Thorpe, *Henry Edwards Huntington: A Biography* (Berkeley: University of California Press, 1994), p. 187.

3. Rufus Steele, "The Red Car of Empire," *Sunset* 31, no. 4 (October 1913).

4. Irving Gill, "The Home of the Future: The New Architecture of the West," *Architect and Engineer* 45, no. 2 (May 1916): 77–86.

5. Nancy Lynn Quam-Wickham, *Petroleocrats and Proletarians: Work, Class, and Politics in the California Oil Industry, 1917–1925* (Ph.D. diss., University of California, Berkeley, 1994), p. 274.

6. Ibid., pp. 280ff.

Chapter Five

1. See, e.g., "A Common-Sense Plan to End Water Shortage," *San Francisco Chronicle*, June 1, 1995.

2. William L. Kahrl, *Water and Power: The Conflict over Los Angeles' Water Supply in the Owens Valley* (Berkeley: University of California Press, 1982), p. 20.

3. See Robert Gottlieb, *Thinking Big: The Story of the Los Angeles Times, Its Publishers, and Their Influence on Southern California* (New York: Putnam, 1977).

4. "Planada: California to Have a Model Municipality," *Architect and Engineer* 25, no. 1 (May 1911): 56–62.

5. Rufus Steele, "The Road to Tomorrow," *Sunset* 32, no. 5 (May 1914): 1038, 1039.

6. William Issel and Robert W. Cherny, *San Francisco, 1865–1932: Politics, Power, and Urban Development* (Berkeley: University of California Press, 1986), p. 63.

7. Frederick Law Olmsted, *The Papers of Frederick Law Olmsted*, vol. 5, *The California Frontier, 1863–1865*, ed. Victoria Post Ranney (Baltimore: Johns Hopkins University Press, 1990), p. 126.

8. Marc Reisner, *Cadillac Desert: The American West and Its Disappearing Water* (New York: Viking, 1986), p. 361.

9. Ibid., pp. 360–73.

10. *Time*, November 18, 1991; April 19, 1993.

11. *San Jose Mercury News*, January 6, 1994.

12. Bob Frost, "Norman Mailer," *San Jose Mercury News, West* magazine, November 17, 1991.

Chapter Six

1. A. J. Wells, "Some California Possibilities," *Out West* 23, no. 4 (October 1905): 347.

2. Promotional brochure, Cypress Lawn Cemetery Association, San Francisco, 1893.

3. O. C. Ellison, "Kern City and the Kern River Oil Districts," *Overland Monthly* 38, no. 1 (July 1901): 71.

4. Robinson Jeffers, *The Selected Poetry of Robinson Jeffers* (New York: Random House, 1959), pp. xv–xvi.

5. Unsigned, "A Christmas Seed Time and a Spring Harvest in the Valley of the San Joaquin, California," *Sunset* 4, no. 4 (February 1900): 155.

6. Mary Austin, "Art Influence in the West," *Century* 89, no. 6 (April 1915): 832.

7. Gerald Haslam, Stephen Johnson, and Robert Dawson, *The Great Central Valley: California's Heartland* (Berkeley: University of California Press, 1993), p. 219.

8. Rachel Carson, *Silent Spring* (Boston, Mass.: Houghton Mifflin, 1962), pp. 1–3.

9. "Study Finds No Drop in State's Birth Defect Rate," *San Francisco Chronicle*, January 24, 1995.

10. "Military Base Cleanups Could Cost $260 Million," *San Francisco Examiner*, November 12, 1992.

11. "Mayor Ties Shipyard's Cleanup to Economy," *San Francisco Chronicle*, December 8, 1993.

12. "Debate over Superfund Listing for Base Sites," *San Francisco Chronicle*, September 25, 1995.

Chapter Seven

1. "Old Ellis Mound to Disappear Soon," *San Francisco Call*, June 21, 1913.

2. W. H. Auden, "September 1, 1939."

3. Frederick Law Olmsted, *The California Frontier, 1863–1865*, ed. Victoria Post Ranney, Vol. 5, *The Papers of Frederick Law Olmsted* (Baltimore: Johns Hopkins University Press, 1990).

4. Ibid., p. 687

5. Ibid., p. 659; Charles Capen McLaughlin, "Olmsted's Odyssey," *Wilson Quarterly* 6, no. 3 (Summer 1982): 83; *California Frontier*, p. 659.

6. *California Frontier*, p. 137.

7. Ibid., p. 3.

8. Michael L. Smith, *Pacific Visions: California Scientists and the Environment, 1850–1915* (New Haven: Yale University Press, 1987), p. 143.

9. Kevin Starr, *Americans and the California Dream, 1850–1915* (New York: Oxford University Press, 1973), p. 162.

10. Stuart Cook, "The Unfulfilled Bay," *California Waterfront Age* 1, no. 4 (Fall 1985): 17.

11. *West County Times*, April 16, 1989.

12. Lewis MacAdams, interview with Gray Brechin, July 12, 1995, Los Angeles.

13. Kevin Stuart and Hans Jenny, "My Friend, the Soil: A Conversation with Hans Jenny," *Journal of Soil and Water Conservation* 39, no. 3 (May–June 1984): 158–61.

The following publications have been important for our understanding of California, its environment, and its social landscape. Much of this list was originally assembled by my wife, Ellen Manchester, as part of our Water in the West Project.

ROBERT DAWSON, 1996

Austin, Mary. "Art Influence in the West." *Century* 89, no. 6 (April 1915): 829–33.

———. *Land of Little Rain.* New York: Ballantine Books, 1971.

Bakker, Elna. *An Island Called California: An Ecological Introduction to Its Natural Communities.* Berkeley: University of California Press, 1971.

Berry, Wendell. *The Unsettling of America: Culture and Agriculture.* San Francisco: Sierra Club Books, 1977.

Beyond Wilderness. Special issue of *Aperture,* no. 120 (Summer 1990).

Bowles, Samuel. *Our New West: Records of Travel between the Mississippi River and the Pacific Ocean.* Bowie, Md.: Heritage Books, 1990.

Bright, Deborah. "Of Mother Nature and Marlboro Men: An Inquiry into the Cultural Meanings of Landscape Photography." *Exposure* 23, no. 4 (1985).

Bronson, William. *How to Kill a Golden State.* Garden City, N.Y.: Doubleday, 1968.

Bryce, James. *The American Commonwealth.* London: Macmillan, 1888.

California Department of Engineering. *Water Resources of Kern River and Adjacent Streams and Their Utilization.* Sacramento: State of California, 1920.

Candee, Hamilton, and Laura King. *The Broken Promise of Reclamation Reform.* San Francisco: Natural Resources Defense Council, October 1987.

Carpenter, Helen M. "Among the Diggers of Thirty Years Ago." *Overland Monthly* 21, no. 124 (April 1893).

Carson, Rachel. *Silent Spring.* Boston, Mass.: Houghton Mifflin, 1962.

Cronon, William. *Nature's Metropolis: Chicago and the Great West.* New York: W. W. Norton, 1991.

Crosby, Alfred W. *Ecological Imperialism: The Biological Expansion of Europe, 900–1900.* New York: Cambridge University Press, 1986.

Crowe, Earle. *Men of El Tejon.* Los Angeles: Ward Ritchie Press, 1957.

Darr, Francis J. A. "Indian Education Applied to the San Carlos Reservation." *Overland Monthly* 5, no. 26 (February 1885): 194–98.

Dasmann, Raymond F. *The Destruction of California.* New York: Macmillan, 1965.

Davis, Mike. *City of Quartz: Excavating the Future in Los Angeles.* London: Verso, 1990.

Derby, George H. "The Topographical Reports of Lieutenant George H. Derby II: Reports on the Tulare Valley of California, April and May,

1850." *Quarterly of the California Historical Society* 11, no. 3 (September 1932): 247–65.

De Voto, Bernard. *The Easy Chair.* Boston: Houghton-Mifflin, 1955.

Didion, Joan. "Letter from Los Angeles." *New Yorker,* February 26, 1990, 87–97.

———. "The Golden Land." *New York Review of Books* 40, no. 17 (October 21, 1993): 85–94.

Donley, Michael W., et al. *Atlas of California.* Culver City, Calif.: Pacific Book Center, 1979.

Eargle, Dolan H., Jr. *The Earth Is Our Mother: A Guide to the Indians of California, Their Historic Locales and Historic Sites.* San Francisco: Trees Company Press, 1986.

Ehrlich, Gretel. *Solace of Open Spaces.* New York: Viking Penguin, 1985.

Ellison, O. C. "Kern City and the Kern River Oil Districts." *Overland Monthly* 38, no. 1 (July 1901): 66–90.

Federal Writers' Project. *The WPA Guide to California: The Federal Writers' Project Guide to 1930's California.* New York: Pantheon Books, 1939.

Foresta, Merry. *Between Home and Heaven: Contemporary American Landscape Photography.* Washington, D.C.: National Museum of American Art, Smithsonian Institution, in association with University of New Mexico Press, Albuquerque, N.M., 1992.

Fradkin, Philip. *A River No More: The Colorado River and the West.* Tucson: University of Arizona Press, 1984.

French, Edgar. "The Re-Discovery of Califor-

nia." *The World's Work* 18, no. 4 (August 1909): 11895–911.

Garner, Van H. *The Broken Ring: The Destruction of the California Indians.* Tucson: Westernlore Press, 1982.

Generating Values in California Real Estate in the 90s: The Newhall Fact Book. Valencia, Calif.: Newhall Land and Farming Company, 1990.

Gottlieb, Robert. *Thinking Big: The Story of the Los Angeles Times, Its Publishers, and Their Influence on Southern California.* New York: Putnam, 1977.

Haslam, Gerald W., and James D. Houston, eds. *California Heartland: Writing from the Great Central Valley.* Santa Barbara, Calif.: Capra Press, 1978.

Haslam, Gerald, Stephen Johnson, and Robert Dawson. *The Great Central Valley: California's Heartland.* Berkeley: University of California Press, 1993.

Hegemann, Werner. *Report on a City Plan for the Municipalities of Oakland and Berkeley.* Oakland: Kelley-Davis Co., 1915.

Heizer, Robert F. *The Destruction of California Indians.* Lincoln: University of Nebraska Press, 1974.

Heizer, Robert F., and Alan J. Almquist. *The Other Californians: Prejudice and Discrimination under Spain, Mexico, and the United States to 1920.* Berkeley: University of California Press, 1971.

Helphand, Kenneth I., and Ellen Manchester. *Colorado: Visions of an American Landscape.* Niwot, Colo.: Roberts Rinehart, 1991.

Hine, Robert V. *California's Utopian Colonies.* New York: W. W. Norton, 1966.

Holing, Dwight. *California Wild Lands: A Guide to the Nature Conservancy Preserves.* San Francisco: Chronicle Books, 1988.

Holliday, J. S. *The World Rushed In: The California Gold Rush Experience.* New York: Simon and Schuster, 1981.

Hoover, Mildred Brooke, Hero Eugene Rensch, Ethel Grace Rensch, and William N. Abeloe. *Historic Spots in California.* 4th ed. Stanford: Stanford University Press, 1990.

Houston, James D. *Californians Searching for the Golden State.* Berkeley, Calif.: Creative Arts Books, 1985.

Hume, Sandy, Ellen Manchester, and Gary Metz, eds. *The Great West: Real/Ideal.* Boulder: University of Colorado, 1977.

Hundley, Norris. *The Great Thirst: Californians and Water, 1770s–1990s.* Berkeley: University of California Press, 1992.

Igler, David. "'When Is a River Not a River?' Reclaiming Nature's Disorder in *Lux v. Haggin*." *Environmental History* 1, no. 2 (April 1996): 52–69.

Issel, William, and Robert W. Cherny. *San Francisco, 1865–1932: Politics, Power, and Urban Development.* Berkeley: University of California Press, 1986.

Jackson, John Brinckerhoff. *Landscapes: Selected Writings of J. B. Jackson.* Amherst: University of Massachusetts Press, 1970.

———. *Changing Rural Landscapes.* Amherst: University of Massachusetts Press, 1977.

Jostes, Barbara Donohoe. *John Parrott, Consul: 1811–1884.* San Francisco, Lawton and Alfred Kennedy, 1972.

Jussim, Estelle, and Elizabeth Lindquist-Cock. *Landscape as Photograph*. New Haven, Conn.: Yale University Press, 1985.

Kahrl, William L. *Water and Power: The Conflict over Los Angeles' Water Supply in the Owens Valley*. Berkeley: University of California Press, 1982.

Kahrl, William L., Steward Brand, et al. *The California Water Atlas*. Sacramento: Governor's Office of Planning and Research, 1979.

Kelley, Robert Lloyd. *Battling the Inland Sea: American Political Culture, Public Policy, and the Sacramento Valley, 1850–1986*. Berkeley: University of California Press, 1989.

Kirkendall, Richard S. "Social Science in the Central Valley of California: An Episode." *California Historical Society Quarterly* 43, no. 3 (September 1964): 195–218.

Klett, Mark. *Revealing Territory: Essays by Patricia Limerick and Thomas W. Southall*. Photographs by Mark Klett. Albuquerque: University of New Mexico Press, 1992.

Klett, Mark, Ellen Manchester, and JoAnn Verburg. *Second View: The Rephotographic Survey Project*. Albuquerque: University of New Mexico Press, 1984.

Kroeber, Theodora. *Ishi in Two Worlds: A Biography of the Last Wild Indian in North America*. Berkeley: University of California Press, 1961.

Kroeber, Theodora, and Robert F. Heizer. *Almost Ancestors: The First Californians*. San Francisco: Sierra Club, 1968.

Kyle, Douglas E. *Historic Spots in California*. Stanford, Calif.: Stanford University Press, 1932.

Lange, Dorothea, and Paul S. Taylor. *An American Exodus: A Record of Human Erosion*. New York: Reynal and Hitchcock, 1939.

Latta, Frank F. *Saga of Rancho El Tejon*. Santa Cruz, Calif.: Bear State Books, 1976.

Liebman, Ellen. *California Farmland: A History of Large Agricultural Landholdings*. Totowa, N.J.: Rowman and Allanhead, 1983.

Lillard, Richard G. *Eden in Jeopardy: Man's Prodigal Meddling with His Environment: The Southern California Experience*. New York: Alfred A. Knopf, 1966.

Limerick, Patricia Nelson. *The Legacy of Conquest: The Unbroken Past of the American West*. New York: W. W. Norton, 1988.

Magee, Thomas. "Overworked Soils." *Overland Monthly* 1 (October 1868).

Margolin, Malcolm. *The Ohlone Way: Indian Life in the San Francisco–Monterey Bay Area*. Berkeley: Heyday Books, 1978.

Mayfield, Thomas Jefferson. *Indian Summer: Traditional Life among the Choinumne Indians of California's San Joaquin Valley*. Berkeley: Heyday Books and California Historical Society, 1993.

McPhee, John. *The Control of Nature*. New York: Farrar, Straus and Giroux, 1989.

———. *Assembling California*. New York: Noonday Press, 1993.

Meinig, D. W., ed. *The Interpretation of Ordinary Landscapes: Geographical Essays*. New York: Oxford University Press, 1979.

Merry, William L. "San Francisco Commerce, Past, Present, and Future." *Overland Monthly* 9, no. 64 (April 1888): 369–74.

Muir, John. *The Mountains of California*. Garden City, N.Y.: Anchor Books, 1961.

Nabhan, Gary Paul, with Mark Klett. *Desert Legends: Re-storying the Sonoran Borderlands*. Text by Gary Paul Nabhan, photographs by Mark Klett. New York: Henry Holt, 1994.

Nabokov, Peter, ed. *Native American Testimony: A Chronicle of Indian-White Relations from Prophecy to the Present, 1492–1992*. New York: Penguin Books, 1992.

Newhall, Ruth Waldo. *A California Legend: The Newhall Land and Farming Company*. Valencia, Calif.: Newhall Land and Farming Company, 1992.

Nordhoff, Charles. *California: For Health, Pleasure, and Residence: A Book for Travellers and Settlers*. Berkeley: Ten Speed Press, 1973.

Norris, Frank. *The Octopus*. New York: Bantam Books, 1963.

Office of Historic Preservation. *California Historical Landmarks*. Sacramento: California Department of Parks and Recreation, 1990.

Olmsted, Frederick Law. *The California Frontier, 1863–1865*. Ed. Victoria Post Ranney. Vol. 5 of *The Papers of Frederick Law Olmsted*. Baltimore: Johns Hopkins University Press, 1990.

Palmer, Tim. *California's Threatened Environment*. Covelo, Calif.: Island Press, 1993.

Pavlik, Bruce M., Pamela C. Muick, Sharon G. Johnson, and Marjorie Popper. *The Oaks of California*. Los Olivos, Calif.: Cachuma Press and the California Oak Foundation, 1991.

Pisani, Donald J. *From the Family Farm to Agribusiness: The Irrigation Crusade in California and the West,*

1850–1931. Berkeley: University of California Press, 1984.

Powers, Stephen. *Tribes of California.* Berkeley: University of California Press, 1976.

Preston, William L. *Vanishing Landscapes: Land and Life in the Tulare Lake Basin.* Berkeley: University of California Press, 1981.

Quam-Wickham, Nancy Lynn. "Petroleocrats and Proletarians: Work, Class, and Politics in the California Oil Industry, 1917–1925." Ph.D. diss., University of California, Berkeley, 1994.

Reisner, Marc. *Cadillac Desert: The American West and Its Disappearing Water.* New York: Viking, 1986.

Reisner, Marc, and Sarah Bates. *Overtapped Oasis: Reform or Revolution for Western Water.* Washington, D.C.: Island Press, 1990.

San Francisco Estuary Project. *Comprehensive Conservation and Management Plan.* Oakland: San Francisco Bay Regional Water Quality Control Board, 1993.

Schoenherr, Allan A. *A Natural History of California.* Berkeley: University of California Press, 1992.

Sheridan, David. *Desertification of the United States.* Washington, D.C.: Council on Environmental Quality, U.S. Government Printing Office, 1981.

Simmons, Ed. *Westlands Water District: The First 25 Years, 1952–1977.* Fresno, Calif.: Westlands Water District, 1983.

Smith, Felix E. "The Kesterson Effect: Reasonable Use of Water and the Public Trust." *San Joaquin Agricultural Law Review* 6, no. 1 (1996): 45–67.

Smith, Michael L. *Pacific Visions: California Scientists and the Environment, 1850–1915.* New Haven, Conn.: Yale University Press, 1987.

Spirn, Anne Whiston. *The Granite Garden: Urban Nature and Human Design.* New York: Basic Books, 1984.

Starr, Kevin. *Americans and the California Dream, 1850–1915.* New York: Oxford University Press, 1973.

Steele, Rufus. "The Red Car of Empire." *Sunset* 31, no. 4 (October 1913): 710–17.

———. "The Road to Tomorrow." *Sunset* 32, no. 5 (May 1914): 1035–39.

Stegner, Wallace. *The American West as Living Space.* Ann Arbor: University of Michigan Press, 1987.

———. *Angle of Repose.* New York: Ballantine Books, 1971.

Stuart, Kevin, and Hans Jenny. "My Friend, the Soil: A Conversation with Hans Jenny." *Journal of Soil and Water Conservation* 39, no. 3 (May–June 1984): 158–61.

Thelander, Carl G. *Life on the Edge: A Guide to California's Endangered Natural Resources: Wildlife.* Santa Cruz, Calif.: Biosystems Books, 1994.

Thompson, Lucy. *To the American Indian.* Berkeley: Heyday Books, 1991.

Thorpe, James. *Henry Edwards Huntington: A Biography.* Berkeley: University of California Press, 1994.

Tuan, Yi-Fu. *Topophilia: A Study of Environmental Perception, Attitudes, and Values.* Englewood Cliffs, N.J.: Prentice Hall, 1974.

Venturi, Robert, Denise Scott Brown, and Steven Izenour. *Learning from Las Vegas: The Forgotten Symbolism of Architectural Form.* Cambridge, Mass.: MIT Press, 1977.

Wells, A. J. "Some California Possibilities." *Out West* 23, no. 4 (October 1905): 345–49.

Williams, James C. *Energy and the Making of Modern California.* Akron, Ohio: University of Akron Press, 1997.

Woehlke, Walter V. "The San Joaquin." *Sunset* 30, no. 3 (March 1913): 219–29.

———. "The Great Valley: A Critical Examination of the Golden State's Economic Backbone." *Sunset* 34, no. 2 (February 1915): 285–96.

Worster, Donald. *Rivers of Empire.* New York: Pantheon Books, 1985.

Zube, Ervin H., and Margaret J. Zube, eds. *Changing Rural Landscapes.* Amherst: University of Massachusetts Press, 1977.

Robert Dawson has received a Visual Artists Fellowship from the National Endowment for the Arts, a Ruttenberg Fellowship from The Friends of Photography, a Dorothea Lange–Paul Taylor Prize from the Center for Documentary Studies at Duke University (with Gray Brechin), and other major awards. His books include *Robert Dawson Photographs* (Tokyo, 1988) and, with Stephen Johnson and Gerald Haslam, *The Great Central Valley: California's Heartland* (Berkeley, 1993). He is founder and codirector with his wife, Ellen Manchester, of the Water in the West Project, a collaboration with other photographers that was published in *Arid Waters: Photographs from the Water in the West Project* (Reno, Nevada, 1992). He has recently completed the Truckee River/Pyramid Lake Project with photographer Peter Goin and writer Mary Webb; a book from that project, *A Doubtful River,* will be published by the University of Nevada Press. He received his B.A. from the University of California at Santa Cruz and his M.A. from San Francisco State University. He currently teaches photography at San Jose State University and Stanford University.

In the 1950s, Gray Brechin watched the Santa Clara Valley go Silicon, and the shock of that transformation never left him. A cofounder of the Mono Lake Committee, Brechin worked in the 1980s as an architectural historian, journalist, lecturer, and television producer in San Francisco, specializing in urban design criticism and environmental issues. With producer Joe Kwong, he helped to break the story of the poisoning of Kesterson National Wildlife Refuge for KQED-TV. His *Imperial San Francisco: Urban Power, Earthly Ruin* (Berkeley, 1999) examines the environmental impact of San Francisco's leading families on the Pacific Basin as an example of what all great cities do to their hinterlands. He recently completed a doctorate in geography at the University of California at Berkeley and has received a Bancroft Fellowship and a Ciriacy-Wantrup Postdoctoral Fellowship to continue his study of the history of mining.

Designer:	Steve Renick
Compositor:	G&S Typesetters, Inc.
Cartographer:	Bill Nelson
Text:	13/17 Centaur
Display:	Syntax
Printer/Binder:	Milanostampa